QUEEN OF GAMES

By the same author
The Style of an Englishman

A HISTORY OF CROQUET

Nicky Smith

Weidenfeld and Nicolson
London

First published in Great Britain in 1991
by George Weidenfeld & Nicolson Ltd
91 Clapham High Street, London SW4 7TA

British Library Cataloguing in Publication Data
Smith, Nicky
    Queen of games : a history of croquet.
    1. Croquet, history
    I. Title
    796.35409

ISBN 0 297 81176 2

Typeset at The Spartan Press Ltd, Lymington, Hants
Printed and bound in Great Britain by
Butler and Tanner Ltd, Frome and London

For Lt.-Col. Ralph Chappell
And all my friends at Compton

Contents

Illustrations

Acknowledgements

T hanks first and foremost to the Croquet Association of Great Britain for permission to print photographs from their collection and for granting access to and the right to quote from the formidable amount of material that they possess. In particular, Brian Macmillan, former Secretary of the CA who patiently unlocked cupboards and laid out precious books for consultation in the CA office at Hurlingham. He was always on hand to answer 'questions from the press' and I very much hope that he will enjoy this book which could not have been completed without his help. Thanks also to Dr Roger Wood for generously entrusting me with volumes from his valuable private collection, notably early croquet editions which provided the older illustrations reproduced here. More special thanks to Charles Townsend, who permitted the reproduction of the register of Hotels and National Register of Official Clubs from his *Croquet Almanack* and to John Walters, Editor of the *Almanack* who provided the photographs of modern players.

In researching this book, I travelled to croquet clubs as far afield as Wellington, New Zealand and interviewed, formally or otherwise, a great many players. Without exception, I was greeted with courtesy and though I cannot list them all, I would like to thank everyone who gave me their time and attention. Those deserving special mention include John Solomon, President of the Croquet Association, Patrick Cotter, former croquet champion and currently bridge correspondent of the *Financial Times* and *Country Life* magazine, Stephen Mulliner, Nigel Aspinall, Professor Bernard Neal, Keith Wylie, Mark Avery, David Openshaw, Phil Cordingly, Bill Lamb, Richard Hilditch, William and Robert Prichard, Robert Fulford and Mark Saurin. From New Zealand, Joe Hogan, Bob Jackson, John Prince and Paul Skinley and from the USA, Jerry Stark, Archie Birchfield, Ted Prentice, Foxy Carter, Tremaine Arkley and Kylie Jones. Also, Bo Harris from Cheltenham, James Kellaway, Colonel Denis Brown, Commander Giles Borrett and Mrs Vera Tyrwhitt-Drake from Compton, Mrs Nora Elvey, Dr Ralph Bucknall from Budleigh Salterton and Dr Roger Bray. I am also deeply indebted to Keith Aiton, official coach to the 1990 Test Team, without whom, much of the 'technical' side of my writing, both here and for the *Financial Times* and *Country Life*, would have been incomplete. I would also like to thank Mrs Aiton for her cheerful willingness to take endless telephone messages.

My greatest debt of gratitude however, is undoubtedly to Mrs D. M. C. Prichard, the Vice-President of the Croquet Association who not only gave me access at Gobion Manor to the many papers which she and her husband had gathered for Colonel Pritchard's *The History of Croquet* but entertained and fed me as well.

Finally, a word of warmest thanks to Peggy, whose constant encouragement and restorative sense of humour helped me overcome those many times when I felt I had taken on too complex a task and that I didn't know a hoop from a handsaw.

INTRODUCTION
Croquet: Queen of Games

C roquet is a splendid game. It is a game which can be played by anyone of any age and does not require great physical strength or expensive outlay on equipment. It is well worth the attention of any person who enjoys a well-organized occupation which allows for a high degree of individual interpretation.

Most people think of croquet as a gentle Victorian pastime, their impressions coloured by Lewis Carroll's famous description of Alice's troublesome game with flamingos, hedgehogs and playing cards. But contemporary croquet is far more than an idle garden game.

Today's top croquet players are often young men at university who play to win. They represent a new kind of croquet, a highly technical and tactical game which is played internationally. Croquet thrives in America, Australia, New Zealand, Canada, South Africa and even Sweden. It is a growing sport on the continent and also in Japan. Yet for all this, it is still a game with an English heart.

Croquet in England has an eventful history which 'officially' begins in the mid-1860s. However, this is not a history book which preoccupies itself with dates and statistics, records and results. Nor is it a book on how to play. A glance at the bibliography will show the reader that there are already a good number of these on the bookshelves as croquet players like nothing better than to analyse the tactics of their sport.

This book is about a game which is essentially a social occupation. It describes the social world of croquet which is the special creation of the people who play, of where they play and, of how they conduct their game. It is a world populated with colourful characters such as George Frederick Handel Elvey a clergyman who always played, rain or shine, in 'fustian black' and Lord Tollemache who wrote a book on croquet containing nearly a hundred photographs of himself playing on his own lawn at Peckforton Castle. Other such characters are C. L. O'Callaghan, known to his friends as 'CL', who spent his summers playing croquet and his winters hunting his way across Ireland or Viscount Doneraile, another Irishman whose favourite food was peach-fed ham and perry and whose other claim to fame was falling into the lake at Hurlingham.

Many croquet clubs are as characterful as the people who formed them and many provide attractive settings for this elegant game. Budleigh Salterton Lawn Tennis and Croquet Club offers views of the sea and a pavilion which echoes the days of the Raj, Cheltenham Croquet Club lies amidst gentle hills and at Compton Croquet Club in East Sussex, the lawns rise in terraces surrounded in springtime by banks of daffodils. Yet nowhere is as grand as Hurlingham, the current 'home' of British croquet. Here the lawns are as flat as table tops and unroll before the imposing facade of the clubhouse like lengths of green baize. Every croquet player hopes to compete at Hurlingham and dreams of winning one of the top championship events which punctuate 'the season' from May to September. But wherever they compete, all croquet players retain happy memories of battles fought like military campaigns though in an atmosphere devoid of strain and hustle, of witnessing both victory and defeat, of forming friendships and sometimes deeper ties and, of food and drink – the treacle tart at Budleigh Salterton, the bygone delight of iced coffee at Hurlingham and the enduring popularity of the bar at Cheltenham.

'Atmosphere' is everything in croquet, whether the game is played at competition level or in a private garden. At home or abroad, croquet inspires a delightful setting. I learnt to play on the (full size) lawn of the British Consulate General in Chiangmai, Northern Thailand. Every evening as the Union Jack slid down the flagpole and the bellow of a water buffalo echoed up from the river to compete with the soft clunk of croquet balls, a servant would appear at the lawnside bearing a silver tray filled with ice-cold drinks.

The Consulate is now closed and I doubt if the croquet lawn, (if it still exists) has been maintained to the same immaculate standard as it was then but it was an unforgettable introduction to this most civilized of games. Ever since, I have wanted to share this sovereign sport by writing about it. The aim of this book then is first and foremost to encourage more people to take up croquet. Secondly, to point the garden player forward to the vast range of possibilities offered by the association game and finally, to capture for all, player and non-player alike, a little of the flavour of the unique blend of skill, settings and social etiquette which together make this the Queen of Games.

THE BRITISH GAME

'*A few years ago, a new game, destined to a great English future was quietly introduced into this country. It had existed for some time in a sort of recreative Bohemia. It had no acknowledged parentage.*'

The Field, *Saturday, 13 August, 1864.*

T wo schools of thought have competed as to how and by whom croquet was actually brought to England. The first established itself in the 1870s and firmly claimed that croquet (spelt with a circumflex on the 'e') was a French game, introduced to England 'during the reign of Charles II when it was played under the name Pall Mall'. The second school of thought dates originally from much the same time but has received more recent endorsement. It states that croquet came to England from Ireland.

Perhaps the most important boost to the 'Pall Mall' theory came from the entry on croquet in the ninth edition of the *Encyclopaedia Britannica*, dated 1877, which claimed croquet as a direct descendant of Pall Mall or 'paille maille'. Many writers on the subject eagerly accepted this authority and expanded on the theory. Some went so far as to claim that the game's 'more remote origin may possibly be traced to Italy; the term Palemaille being in accordance with the Italian Palamaglio, from palla, a ball and maglio, a mallet'. Others referred to the diarist Samuel Pepys who recorded on 2 April 1661, that he

1

had seen for the first time the game of Pelemele played in St James's Park.

H. F. Crowther Smith, a croquet player and author of several books on the subject including *The Art of Croquet* published in 1932, certainly settled for paille maille as 'a fairly secure source of the game'. However a more recent authority, D. M. C. Prichard, reached the conclusion that in fact the two games simply shared a common ancestry. He further pointed out that the nineteenth-century croquet enthusiast Dr Richard Prior, who exhaustively discussed the possibility of the game's descent from paille maille in a much quoted publication in 1872, concluded that paille maille was in fact, very different to croquet.

Even so, it seems reasonable to assume that there is an historical link between the French game of paille maille and modern croquet though quite how the game came to be introduced into England is a different matter. Despite the theories involving Charles II and the games he introduced from France, the most acceptable view is that croquet came to England from Ireland.

A possible story of croquet's introduction to England involves a certain Miss Macnaughton (at other times referred to as 'Miss Macausland') who is said to have brought the game to Ireland from northern France, where it was played with broomsticks and hoops made from willow rods. A more refined game of crooks and balls seems to have been quite popular in northern France well into the present century. Indeed, Maurice Reckitt, a former chairman of the Croquet Association, croquet's governing body, who wrote an unpublished history of croquet in the Sixties, claimed to have a postcard illustrating such a game being played on the beaches of Brittany. Arthur Lillie, one of croquet's earliest chroniclers, had also seen croquet played in France at the turn of the century and wrote a detailed description of the experience (see p.35).

Miss Macnaughton is said to have given the idea to a Mr Spratt of Hanover Square who passed it on to John Jaques of Hatton Garden. A more likely version of this story is that Jaques himself saw the game in Ireland and brought back the idea. He was credited with the accomplishment in an exceedingly long poem which first appeared in *Punch* in July 1864 the opening lines of which pro-claimed:

'Whence croquet sprang to benefit the earth
What happy garden gave the pastime birth,
What cunning craftsman carved its graceful tools
Whose oral teaching fixed its equal rules,
Sing Jaques thou apostle of the game!
If dissyllabic is thy famous name
Or if, as Frenchified, it is but one
By saying "Sing John Jacques" the trick is done.'

More to the point, Arthur Lillie, in his book, published in 1897, quotes from a letter written to him by Jaques in 1873, in which the latter states in a footnote that he made his first croquet set from patterns he found in Ireland while there on a business trip and that, 'I made the implements and published directions (such as they were) before Mr Spratt introduced the subject at all to me.'

Lillie quotes his contemporary Dr Prior, on the Miss Macnaughton story and adds his own piece of research in the form of a letter from the lady's sister which stated that, 'croquet . . . was played in northern France and was introduced by some Irish family to Ireland a long time ago. My brother wrote out the rules about fifteen or twenty years ago and gave them to Mr Spratt, who very quickly spread their fame. Until the rules were written it had been played from tradition, and the mallets made by country carpenters.' In support of this, *Land and Water* announced in the 18 December edition of 1869 that 'We have received from Mr Spratt of Brook Street and print below, the first published rules of croquet given to him by Miss Macnaughton in 1851.'

No doubt the Miss Macnaughton story and Jaques' own version as told to Arthur Lillie both contain elements of the truth.

A variation on the former story was given by Prichard's wife Elizabeth in *Playing Fields*, the Journal of the National Playing Fields Association in the January–March edition of 1972, in which she wrote that a group of travellers from Ireland saw the men of a village in Brittany playing a game on the beach 'with bent willow rods for hoops and crooks called "croquets"'. Elizabeth Prichard went on to explain how these travellers subsequently introduced croquet 'or re-introduced it' into Ireland before offering it for sale around London where Spratt bought the set from them, then sold it to Jaques.

Whatever the real order of proceedings, it does seem that the game came to England from Ireland. On this point, Dr Prior was quite adamant. 'Who invented croquet, or who improved a rustic game into one fit for polite society, is a question that has often been asked and has never been answered. One thing only is certain: it is from Ireland that it came to England, and it was on the lawn of the late Lord Lonsdale that it was first played in this country.'

One may add with equal conviction that it was John Jaques who had a leading role in popularizing the game in England. Jaques produced his first comprehensive code of laws in 1864 although he appears to have published a first edition about 1857 followed by a new edition about 1860.

As to the origins of the word 'croquet' there are many theories. An article in *The Queen* on 28 June 1862 signed by 'J. Hooker' offered the following explanation: 'I believe the word croquet to be French and to belong to the class of words which, both in French and in English, express their meaning by their sound, as crick-crack means a rending or cracking noise, tintin, the jingling of glasses, tintamarre, a regular hullabaloo . . . In the French, 'roquer' means to castle, which we need scarcely say is to place the castle by the side of the king and pass the king to the other side of it.' Another early theory held that the name derives from the French words *croquer le marmot*, signifying 'to dance attendance upon'.

A few years later, Lillie quoted the Rev J. G. Wood at some length. 'The word croquet is derived from a French word *croquer*, to crunch with the teeth. This word is used to describe the sound caused by eating anything very hard and brittle. There is a sort of gingerbread made in France which is very thin, hard and brittle and is called croquet in allusion to the sound produced in eating it. The word is used to distinguish the game in consequence of the crackling sound of the mallets against the ball.'

Lillie dismissed all this as 'nonsense', saying that 'the croquet was the instrument that was used by French peasants' but many years later, Prichard cheerfully scorned the translation of 'croquet' into 'crook'. Saying he could not find this latter word in his French dictionary, he wrote 'which defines the word "croquet" as "a cross, irritable man"!' Another modern theory has argued that the word croquet was a derivative of the Gallic *cluiche*, meaning 'to play'.

The reader is at liberty to make a choice. Whatever the origin of the word, croquet as a garden game had become all the rage in the 1860s. It had also begun to acquire its dangerous reputation. An article in *The*

Queen in September 1865 observed that 'Croquet is found by experience to rouse the angry passions of old ladies'.

By 1867, John Jaques, who had become recognized as something of an authority on croquet, had printed 65,000 copies of his *Laws and Regulations* and the game was widely accepted 'as a popular pastime of a very light and easy description at garden parties'. The reason most commonly cited for this sudden surge of interest is that in an age of chaperoned females, croquet provided the opportunity for both sexes to indulge in a little light flirtation. This may also have contributed to croquet's early 'reputation' for as one commentator later noted, 'Where there is any prejudice against the game, it is due to the memory retained of the absurdly wide hoops, small mallets and balls used at that time which gave it a philandering atmosphere and affected it in public opinion as a game of little importance.'

However croquet was not the only Victorian pastime which offered scope for a little 'philandering'. A frivolous poem by Clement Scott, repeated from the pages of *Fun* magazine by Walter Jones Whitmore in his *Croquet Tactics* published in 1868, makes it clear that rowing and dancing provided equally good opportunities for daytime 'spooning'. The Rev. Francis Kilvert, whose diary gives a detailed picture of life in rural England in mid-Victorian times makes frequent reference to the croquet parties he attended. Most seem to have combined both croquet and archery and the genteel atmosphere of afternoon games, in the company of a variety of young ladies, starkly contrasted with Kilvert's descriptions of the activities of the poorer classes, many of whom it seems, spent their nights lying by the roadside 'drunk, cursing, muttering, maundering and vomiting'.

No doubt, the pleasant game of croquet also endeared itself to hostesses of country house parties because it could simultaneously entertain a large group. In those days, it was usually played by eight people or sometimes as many as sixteen. This explains the early pictures of the game where crowds of people seem to be nonchalantly strolling about the court. It is also reflected a little in the atmosphere of fluster and confusion which Carroll expressed in his description of Alice's game.

While not quite involving flamingos or hedgehogs, the equipment of these early games seems quite extraordinary. The lawns were large with no boundaries. The hoops were also large, nearly a foot wide and thirteen inches high and rounded at the top like arches. They were laid out, eight or ten of them at a time, in a sort of diamond pattern, or a hexagon, with extra hoops at top and bottom, and there were two pegs, generally set one at each end, one used for starting and the other for turning. In contrast to the hoops, the mallets were tiny, only a few inches in length, but equally oddly shaped. Some were cylindrical others wedge-shaped and all only about four-and-a-half inches long. They were made from boxwood and sometimes ivory and, according to Jaques, the handles were Malacca cane, American hickory or English ash.

Croquet as a simple social pastime gradually waned but thanks to the enthusiasm of a few players, the game was also taken up as a competitive one. The man most responsible for this was Walter Jones Whitmore.

The son of a Cotswold landowner called John Henry Whitmore, who changed his name to Whitmore Jones when he inherited, Walter later changed the name again to Jones Whitmore. It was one of the milder eccentricities of a man who seemed to have had many passions in life, the most enduring of which was undoubtedly croquet. He started playing about 1860 and a few years later, began writing on the game in the pages of *The Field*. In 1866, the magazine published a series of articles on tactics by Walter and also a set of rules and in 1867 he had the great idea of organizing a croquet tournament.

This event, which took place on a bowling green at Evesham in Worcestershire is now recognized as the first Open Championship of the modern game of croquet. The main excitement of the tournament was that Walter himself won, despite the fact that one of the other players created an uproar by appearing with a mallet that was five inches long. The hoops were eight inches wide and at least two of the players used one-handed mallets with handles made of cane. The contestants seem to have been few in number and mostly drawn from among Walter's close friends but the competition was successful enough to encourage another the following year.

This time, the tournament was held on a cricket ground at Moreton-in-Marsh and on a somewhat grander scale. It was advertised in *The Field* with an entry fee of one guinea. Admission to the ground was one shilling per ticket for each person plus an extra shilling for each carriage. Arthur Lillie describes how 'the excellent inn, the White Hart, had to stretch itself to put up this good company'. Other players lived locally. Mr Arthur Law, for example, rode over from his parish of Chipping Camden.

It was an exciting tournament demonstrating some excellent play. Walter won his first round against Mr G. A. Muntz but was beaten in the final by his cousin, Walter Peel. Lillie describes the highlights of the match:

'First game – there was fine play on both sides, Mr Whitmore being very brilliant at one time though his longest break was but seven points . . . Second game – Mr Peel early in the game all but made a very long shot. He afterwards got in and played three fine breaks all in favour of one ball, taking it to the last hoop which he declined. Then Mr Whitmore came in by a magnificent shot from corner to corner, forty-eight yards . . . when he had reached nearly the same score as Mr Peel, the latter got in by a good shot at thirty yards and never gave his adversary another chance. Third game . . . Mr Peel obtained the first break and played brilliantly. Mr Whitmore on coming in also played well . . . Mr Peel got in by a very fine shot at thirty-five yards, and followed it up by very fine play, keeping the break after missing a rather difficult hoop by a roquet at twenty-four yards. He then took the balls home the same break.'

The tournament was written up in at least two publications and *The Field* sent its special correspondent, Henry Jones, or 'Cavendish', who was a self-styled expert, having given up a career as a surgeon to take up the post as writer. (The then editor of *The Field*, J. H. Walsh was also a surgeon who had become very interested in sport.) Henry Jones was the author of the entry on croquet in the ninth edition of the *Encyclopaedia Britannica* referred to above and also of *The Pocket Book of Croquet* which was roundly criticized by other 'authorities' on the subject.

Jones was a founder member of the All England Croquet Club (AECC) which held its first meeting in the offices of *The Field* in 1868. Walter Jones Whitmore was elected as secretary and was deputed to go and search for a suitable site on which to establish a club. The next three years were fraught with internal squabbles and power struggles. Walter's attempts at finding premises proved unsuccessful and disappointing. At one stage, he had hoped for amalgamation with the Royal Toxopholite Society but at the last moment they withdrew from the agreement. 'I must say I consider they have acted very badly towards me. This gives me all my work to begin again,' he wrote to

Dr Prior. The search also proved costly and as time went by, Walter increasingly fell out with his other committee members over the question of finance. In 1869, he entered into a strident correspondence with the All England Croquet Club, indignantly listing the charges against himself. 'It is said 1) That I failed to obtain a ground in London, 2) That it was my intention to use my position as Secretary as a means of pecuniary profit to myself, 3) That I altered and falsified the minutes.' Poor Walter. Inevitably, he was dismissed from his post as secretary that same year but, undeterred, he continued in opposition and eventually became secretary of a splinter group which called itself the National Croquet Club (NCC). Still in contention with most of his acquaintances, Walter seems to have begun to appreciate that his influence was waning for in 1870 he wrote to a former colleague, 'You take it for granted that I have absolute power over the Committee which is not the case.'

Walter and Henry Jones who remained with the original committee, broke into open warfare with Whitmore writing furious letters to both *The Field* and *Land and Water*, threatening legal action. Jones was no doubt encouraged by his editor, J. H. Walsh, who also quarrelled with Walter. The debate raged on between the two rival groups, hindering all attempts at producing a codified set of rules, but by 1870 it seemed that the original AECC had secured the upper hand.

For a start, they had found a ground. Four acres of land were leased to them by a Wimbledon solicitor. This was to later be the headquarters of lawn tennis until the club moved from Worple Road to Church Road in 1922. In July 1870, they held their first championship meeting in which members of the rival NCC also took part. The Championship was won by Walter Peel but led to bitter allegations by Walter Jones Whitmore that during their game together, his cousin had cheated.

Walter once again found himself eased out of a croquet committee and once again he formed his own. The main achievement of this new Grand National Croquet Club was a tournament held in Aldershot (see p.30) but the GNCC seems to have dissolved a year later when Walter died in 1872.

Prichard gives a very precise account of these early struggles to codify a set of laws for croquet and concludes with a somewhat damning picture of Walter as clever but lacking in judgement, inventive but impractical, 'full of energy and ambitious but content to idle away much of his time at Chastleton'.

Visitors to the Cotswolds would do well to take a little time to visit Chastleton. A rare example of a Tudor manor house, it stands on top of a little rise. Honey-coloured stone, tidy proportions and two jaunty weathervanes flying from each end of matching square towers, add to its attraction as a country gentleman's home. It has all the embellishments of a small castle but none of the pomposity. It is now inhabited by members of the Clutton-Brock family but it boasts many historical legends including one which claims that Charles II (who apparently learned the game of croquet in France) took refuge here after his defeat at Worcester. Arthur Lillie claimed to have slept in a bedroom which gave access to a secret chamber where escapees from Cromwell's Ironsides took refuge but happily, he 'was not disturbed by any ghost'. Various croquet chroniclers have visited the house and been somewhat dismayed at the confusion of letters written in Walter's cramped neurotic handwriting which lie scattered amidst the copies of his *Croquet Tactics*. No doubt they are of little interest to the general public though they provide a fascinating insight into his own obsessive character and show that far from idling away his time, Walter spent much of it in heated correspondence.

Next door to the house lies a small church and a churchyard. It is mostly filled with the graves of two important families, the Newmans and Clutton-Brocks. Only two memorials to the family of Whitmore Jones are identifiable, one of them a simple but vast wooden cross with a small bronze plaque nailed to it, the other a barely legible headstone. The Church is Norman in its oldest part – and, at the time of writing, desperately in need of funds for repairs. In a corner of the right aisle is a marble memorial plaque. It lists first John Henry Whitmore Jones, Walter's father 'second son of William Whitmore of Dudmaston in the County of Salop. He succeeded to the estate of Chastleton on the death of Arthur Jones Esq, 1828.' Then come the names of John Henry's wife Dorothy and three of their sons – 'John Arthur Whitmore Jones, son and heir of the above (who died) 1857, aged 35 years, William Whitmore Jones, their second son, January 1874, aged 47 years, Wolryche Harry Whitmore Jones, their fourth son, August 1874, aged 36 years' and finally, their eldest daughter Mary Elizabeth, who considering the short lives of some of her brothers lived to an incredible ninety-one.

Walter's name is conspicuously missing from this family memorial but to the left of it, high on a facing wall, a grimy bronze plaque carries the just distinguishable words:

'In Memory of Walter Thomas
Third son of John Henry Whitmore Esq.
and his wife Dorothy
who died July 27th 1872
Aged 41 years.'

In its neglected state, this small plaque is a poignant memorial to the man who is now acknowledged as 'the father of modern croquet'. It represents a sad end (he died of cancer of the throat) to a life filled with the frustrations and dissatisfaction of a man who tried his hand at many things but perfected few of them.

Walter was a 'character'. A difficult, inconsistent person more given to taking up new schemes than to seeing them through, an 'ideas' man rather than an adminstrator. Lillie describes how he loved a 'finicking game and timid, finicking maxims'. For all that, his contribution to croquet was profound and lasting. He had saved the game from near extinction by emphasizing its intellectual possibilities and encouraging other enthusiasts to help him establish it as a competitive sport. Much of his technical advice in his small book *Croquet Tactics*, is relevant today and as Lillie recognized more than a century ago, 'He was the first to show in print that the introduction of loose croquet had in point of fact given birth to a new and distinct pastime, a game of subtle and beautiful combinations'. But Walter had also set the game off on the long debate which still echoes down the years between those who see croquet as a social affair and those who regard it as a business.

Meanwhile, despite the internal wranglings of the committees governing croquet in the late 1860s, the game was flourishing. Articles appeared regularly in *Land and Water* and *The Field*, many of them remarkably similar to those which appear today in *Croquet*, the magazine of the Croquet Association, covering points of law and debating tactics. The next few years saw the introduction of regular tournaments and hoops gradually became smaller while balls and mallets increased in size. J. H. Hale, one of the original members of the founding committee of the AECC introduced a new setting with only six hoops. He is also credited with being the inventor of a heavy mallet with a lignum vitae head, called The Cavendish.

Croquet was in its heyday with numerous tournaments and ladies enjoying the game as much as men. But this success was to be shortlived.

In 1874, a Major Wingfield patented a bat and ball game he called 'sphairistike'. 'Sticky' as it became known, soon changed its name to the more elegant 'Lawn Tennis' and its popularity mushroomed overnight. Lawns which had been constructed at feverish pace for croquet were as rapidly turned into tennis courts. So much so, that there is some cause for speculation that tennis might not have had such a rapid success if these lawns had not been so readily to hand. That said, it should also be acknowledged that the rules for croquet were complicated and constantly open to reinterpretation, indeed as they still are, while tennis was a comparatively simple game.

The croquet committee at Wimbledon unwittingly helped the transformation by agreeing to set aside a lawn for tennis and badminton. Only a few years later, in 1877, the change was confirmed when the first tennis championships were held at Wimbledon and the AECC changed its name to the All England Croquet and Lawn Tennis Club. Croquet slid into decline.

Lawn tennis was taken up everywhere and by everyone, including the press. With the perfidy of those only interested in the 'latest news', J. H. Walsh and Henry Jones of *The Field* embraced the new faith and turned against croquet. Jones went so far as to propose that prize meetings be discontinued at Wimbledon and that the word 'croquet' be deleted altogether from the club's title. Despite several rearguard attempts to ward off the inevitable (most of them fought out in the Charing Cross Hotel, which, as Prichard notes, was an early battle-ground for croquet meetings of a critical nature) the proposal to change the title and 'to abolish public competitions for croquet prizes at Wimbledon' was carried, though members were still allowed to take part in private games. However, even this seems to have been discouraged but an order to destroy the croquet records was thwarted by a groundsman who, legend has it, hid them until better times returned. It was not until 1899 that the club once again changed the title to become the All England Lawn Tennis and Croquet Club (AELTC) – which is how it remains today.

But if croquet at Wimbledon was now outmoded, it continued to be played in some country homes and in a few clubs.

Chief among these were Cheltenham and Budleigh Salterton but smaller clubs also played a part. In 1956, writing in croquet's official publication then called the Croquet Gazette, G. F. Handel Elvey, of whom more later, remembered a club at Ascot Heath where Lt.-Col.

the Hon. H. Needham lived. (The latter became Secretary of the AELTC in 1897.) 'In his recruiting efforts for the (Ascot Heath) Club, he persuaded my mother to join,' wrote the Rev. Elvey. 'My mother, wanting some practice, asked me to play with her at our old home, The Towers, Windlesham. Previously I had no interest in games but from the start croquet gripped me.'

He goes on to describe several of the great players of the day, including Arthur Law who played against Walter Whitmore Jones in the Evesham tournament and Arthur Lillie, another player-writer who 'went over from Cheltenham with the Rev. Arthur Law to watch the latter play at Evesham.'

Rev. Elvey writes that Mr Law 'was a man of medium height with a pretty thick shock of hair, and played the old across-the-body stroke. He held his mallet very firmly with the forefinger of his right hand down the shaft.' In contrast, 'Mr Arthur Lillie was a thin, tallish man, and played what we now call the side style and I remember he had some sort of knob and thickened part at the end of his mallet.'

From this reminiscence of his early days at croquet, the Rev. Elvey concludes that the period between the last Championship in 1882 and croquet's revival in 1897 'was not so complete a break as is sometimes supposed'. It may not have had the following it had enjoyed in the 1860s, but croquet was still played at tournament level. Fortunately, it also appears to have had some friends in the more popular world of lawn tennis.

Notable among these was B. C. Evelegh whom Elvey remembers as a 'well-known Lawn Tennis Referee, and who also played croquet under his christian name of Bonham-Carter'. Evelegh, who was twice croquet Open Champion persuaded the AELTC to set aside one lawn at Wimbledon for croquet and in 1896, he further persuaded them to give up their tennis lawns to stage a week's croquet tournament.

This was the United All England Croquet Association (UAECA) Gold Medals. The rather grand name had been thought up by Walter Peel, three times winner of the Open Championships in the 1860s and 1870s who no longer played much. However, in 1896 he invited all the well-known croquet players to compete for the new title.

There were separate tournaments for both ladies and gentlemen and the former was won by a Miss Maud Drummond, daughter of an ex-army officer who had served in India and had a lawn at his house at Petworth in Sussex.

The men's medal was won by C. E. Willis (later famous as the man who introduced the single peg setting which came into use in 1922). Rev. Elvey records that Willis played 'with a short yellow mallet' and that he was a marvellous shot.

In 1896, tournaments were held at Budleigh Salterton, Bristol, Bath and Eastbourne and a year later, the AELTC relented and the Opens and Ladies Championships were revived at Wimbledon.

Meanwhile, the laws had been consistently revised. Lt.-Col. Needham records in his book *Croquet* that 'Mr Evelegh had revised Laws and Regulations published in 1894 and 1895 and in 1895 and 1896, Mr W. H. Peel's Association Laws appeared.' Needless to say, there was some confusion, or as Needham tactfully put it, 'considerable scope for a variety of opinion on certain points'. In 1897, the committee of the UAECA produced the official 'Laws of Croquet'. The following year they produced regulations for prize meetings and finally, in 1899, they incorporated the two into a single edition.

The headquarters of croquet at the time seem to have been peripatetic. They moved first to Sheen, near Richmond Surrey, then to Roehampton. By 1900, the UAECA had shortened its name to the Croquet Association (CA), which is how it is called today and the game was well and truly resuscitated.

The Sportman's Year Book for 1899 records: 'It is no longer apt to speak of Croquet as a reviving game. It is emphatically revived, and the last season has shown it to be in a thoroughly healthy condition. Without a suspicion of "mania", there is a keen interest taken in the game, an interest which finds its best organized and developed form in the South and West of England.'

Croquet's star was once again in the ascendant and it continued to shine throughout the Edwardian era. It was played by those with time and money, time for week-long tournaments and money for large country houses which hosted a constant round of seasonal parties. This was considered the 'golden age' of croquet when elegant women wore picture hats and pretty dresses and dapper men sported suits, with panamas or flat caps.

'The boom in croquet is phenomenal,' wrote Lt.-Col. Needham at the turn of the century. 'The number of Associates has risen steadily in four years to between five- and six-hundred, with every indication of continued increase. All over the country clubs crop up and thrive. The Colonies have caught the craze, and wherever the Union Jack flies there may the tell-tale tap be heard.' His enthusiasm hints of the 'mania' abhorred by others but it seems to have been borne out by advertisements which appeared in the Croquet Gazette, first published in 1904, referred to hereafter as 'the gazette'.

Players were obviously undeterred by weather as this small item in the 'Sales, Wants and Exchange Column' testifies: 'Wanted, Associates to send their dyeing and cleaning to the Royal Sutton Cleaning Works, Warwickshire. Ladies' Blouses a speciality; just the thing after a wet week's tournament.'

Houses were also advertised to let. 'Kessingland Grange. Stands in its own private grounds of about ten acres overlooking sea . . . two full-sized croquet grounds, stabling for three horses and good coachhouse.' This establishment also boasted four sitting rooms, two halls, sixteen beds and dressing rooms and domestic offices. There was, however, only one bathroom with hot and cold water.

Bright among the rising stars of this period were the Irish. Three young men and one woman, Miss Nina Coote, invaded croquet. The men soon became known as the 'Irish Terrors', winning all before them.

They seem to have been a likeable trio. The leader was Cyril Corbally, a tall, slim, angular chap, supposedly of a delicate constitution but a brilliant tactician. He won the Open Championship five times between 1902 and 1913 and according to Rev. Elvey, was 'the greatest exponent of centre play'. Elvey also remembers Corbally's 'long sensitive fingers', for like his other two compatriots, Corbally held his mallet in the 'Irish grip'. One of his victories in the Open Championships was against C. L. O'Callaghan who went on to win three times. He looks a handsome man in the old photographs that remain, having the brooding appearance of a rather unpredictable character. He led the life of a dashing country squire, hunting his way across Ireland during the winter, pausing only in summer to play croquet. Reporting on a Championship in 1923, the then editor of the gazette noted with some surprise 'Captain C. L. O'Callaghan reclining comfortably among the spectators and occasionally handling meditatively two white golf balls!' He went on, 'Captain O'Callaghan is one of the few first-class players who can make even a monotonous four-ball-break look attractive, and his desertion from the ranks of competitors was a serious loss. We are glad to report that he told us he had not given up croquet and would probably be playing later on in the season.' In fact, he soon after took to golf completely and never played croquet again.

The third member of this triumvirate was P. 'Duff' Mathews, known as 'the Duffer' who won the Open Championships four times before returning to Ireland to take up farming. A boyish looking character, he seems to have rarely appeared without a cigarette in his mouth. He was much liked and all three of the 'Irish Terrors' attracted great interest whenever they appeared at tournaments, whether they played or not.

Croquet was gaining in strength and by 1914, the Association could boast 170 registered clubs with over 2,300 members. The gazette, reflected this boom with articles on new clubs and lists of tournaments throughout the season, including mention of those on the French Riviera where players could continue the game throughout the winter. Then came the war.

There is no doubt that croquet, as much as everything else in Edwardian life, was affected though at first, it seemed as if nothing had changed. Tournaments continued to be announced throughout 1914 but the practice declined when it became known that too many people considered it in poor taste. 'Rolls of Honour' soon appeared instead, along with lists of players in active service abroad. A letter published in the gazette in 1915 received from a Dr Pepper, recorded the misery of war saying 'There has been desperate hand-to-hand fighting in this village, (in Northern France) the place having been taken and re-taken several times. There is not a whole house standing, and there are trenches running through what were once people's drawing rooms.' The writer comments at length on the necessity of trying to keep dry in the trenches, which, in the midst of all the horror and discomfort, reminded him of nothing less than playing croquet in the wet.

Individual membership to the Association fell to 1,400 and several clubs which closed their doors at the start of the war, never reopened them.

For all that, croquet revived almost immediately after the war and went on to even greater strength in the Twenties and Thirties. By 1923, the pages of the gazette are full of fixtures, notes on payment of subscriptions (then one pound) and advertisements for Menton, Costabelle and the Hyeres Croquet Club 'with the six best lawns in the South of France'. A tournament at Woking between 30 April and 5 May records an entry of nearly forty, including several first-class players – very gratifying for so early in the season. That year, *The Bystander* commented in somewhat merry vein: 'Croquet is now a highly scientific business, played by scientists of both sexes. The men and women who reach the higher hoops, as it were, are obviously people of another world to the frivolous weekend one such as yours and mine. Champions were pointed out to me reverently. Bearded men with detached expressions, who thought of the game in terms of higher mathematics.'

Croquet was at last becoming properly codified and in terms of the game itself, this was the real 'golden age'. The game was full of exciting players, both male and female, some of whom, like Duff Mathews, returned to the courts after the war as easily as if they had never left. Tournaments were flourishing, membership to the Association was steadily rising again (by 1930 it stood at 1,700) and, perhaps most important of all, foundations for the present game were finally being firmly laid.

The adoption of the single peg 'Willis setting' has already been referred to. In addition, the 'either ball game' finally replaced the old-fashioned method of playing the colours in sequence. Bisques were introduced to give extra turns to those with long handicaps and the principle of the 'lift' was established at Championship level to give the out-player a better chance of getting in. The three and three-quarter-inch hoop was reintroduced which, along with the Willis setting, helped make the game more challenging. A Mens' Championship was inaugurated but even more exhilarating, croquet went truly international with the first ever Test match against Australia, played at Roehampton in July 1925.

'Dull and cheerless weather' marked the first contest for this event, known as the MacRobertson Shield and named after a sweet manufacturer (see p.20). Even so, some 200 spectators turned up for the final which was won by the British team. 'One need hardly say that in the matter of Test matches the home side holds always a strong advantage in that they are free to select as they please from the entire stock of their playing strength,' commented the gazette. Rather prophetically as it turned out, for the British lost when they sent a team to Australia in 1928 and again in 1935. On this last occasion, New Zealand joined in to make it a triangular series.

The Thirties saw a return to troubled times and squabbling in croquet's internal affairs. Once again, the problem was one of economics and the subject of finances rumbled back and forth while membership slowly slipped to stand at 1,350 in 1939. This time, when war broke out there was no hesitation. Play ceased abruptly.

Croquet was kept alive during the Second World War under the central guidance of the Croquet Association, organized by the Rev. Elvey who was determined to keep things ticking over with low subscriptions and strict economies. A few clubs, like Cheltenham, Budleigh Salterton and Roehampton remained active, others, like Blackheath were bombed out of existence or like Bude, Stevenage and Winchester, simply faded away.

This time there was no sudden resurrection. Many of the great players of the Thirties were either dead or disabled by illness. The Hurlingham Club, which before the war had been famous as the headquarters for British polo, had been partly requisitioned and now faced an attempt to nationalize it.

From the end of the Second World War to the early Sixties, play was dominated by three men – Patrick Cotter, John Solomon and Humphrey Hicks but in the early Sixties, the field once again began to widen when a group of young undergraduates entered a tournament in Roehampton.

In 1967, Hurlingham celebrated the hundredth anniversary of the first Open Championship. So much had happened in the game since Walter Jones Whitmore organized his first tournament at Evesham in 1867. Croquet had waxed and waned in popularity, experienced periods of stability followed by disarray and taken longer than almost any other game, to establish itself on the international scene. (Lawn Tennis, held its first international competition in 1905). In some ways, the history of croquet's development in Britain mirrors the game itself. Never predictable, full of high and low spots, moments of great euphoria followed by seemingly irreversible setbacks. But as Walter Jones Whitmore wrote, 'The game is never lost till it is won.' Down the years the thought has pulled many a player through to final victory.

The future now looks bright again and increasing numbers of younger players have brought new vitality to the game. In 1989 the first official world championships were won by New Zealander Joe

Hogan. A year later, a twenty-one-year-old university student, Robert Fulford, gave Britain its first official world champion. Today croquet is well established as an international sport.

THE DEVELOPMENT OF
CROQUET WORLDWIDE

N ewcomers to croquet are often surprised to learn that it is an international game, yet Test matches have been played between Great Britain, New Zealand and Australia since 1925. In 1986 Great Britain took part in the first world invitational series in the USA, a delegation was sent to Japan to demonstrate the game and discussion opened on the formation of a World Croquet Federation. In 1989, the first World Singles Championships were played at Hurlingham.

Australia, New Zealand, the USA, Canada, England, Wales, Scotland, Ireland and Japan competed, while France and Italy sent observers. The same year saw the inaugural meeting of the World Croquet Federation and croquet was also included as a demonstration sport in the World Games at Karlsruhe in Germany. The Test countries are as follows:

Australia

Croquet was introduced to both Australia and New Zealand by settlers in the mid-nineteenth century. In Australia, the game was largely played on private lawns and seems to have first taken hold in Victoria. The south-eastern mainland state of Australia has a temperate climate with a high rainfall which dictates that the croquet season runs, much as the British one, from May to September. The earliest record of croquet in Australia dates from 1866 with mention of the Kyneton Club in rural Victoria, the first of many croquet clubs to be established throughout the Australian Continent.

In 1914, the Victorian Croquet Association was the first state association to be founded, followed by the South Australia Croquet Association, the New South Wales Croquet Player's Association, the Queensland Croquet Association and, in 1928, the Western Australia Croquet Association and the Tasmanian Croquet Association on the small island state at the southern tip of the mainland. Tasmania is known as the 'Apple Isle' and has a climate much like England's which allows the cultivation of bent grass instead of the tougher couch grass which predominates throughout much of the rest of Australia's croquet clubs.

The reasons for croquet's early popularity in Australia are uncertain. Perhaps it reminded the early settlers of home. More likely, it was simply appreciated as a good game. As Prichard remarked, croquet proliferated 'like that other immigrant, the rabbit'.

In 1916, an article in the gazette noted that croquet in Victoria 'has during the last year or so made a distinct advance, and is now regarded as being established, and admitted to the same standing as bowls, lawn tennis, golf and other thoroughly recognized sports'. This, the article went on to say, was the result of the formation of the Victorian Croquet Association which had attracted 'for its direction and management prominent players and several experienced businessmen who take an active and valued interest in its administration'.

So confident was the new Association that in 1919, it invited Britain to send a team to visit Australia. The 'home guard' were caught unawares, not only by the unexpectedness of the invitation but by the fact that war had recently ended and reconstruction in England was still slowly taking place. In contrast, croquet in Australia seemed to have carried on much as usual. The attempt to put together a British team soon floundered but the Australians remained undaunted. In 1925, they sent a team to England.

They were encouraged by an Australian millionaire who had made his money through sweet manufacturing. Sir Macpherson Robertson presented a trophy for international competition which became known as the MacRobertson Shield. This series of tests, played every four years in each of the three countries in turn, is the croquet equivalent of the Davis Cup. All three countries have won the trophy on different occasions and competition is usually of a very high standard. So far, the USA has not participated but there are definite plans afoot for them to be included soon.

The first of the series of three Test matches took place at Roehampton Club on Friday and Saturday, 26 and 27 June 1925. The Australians had brought over only five players while England had the advantage of being able to select as they pleased from their playing strength. On this occasion, the team included D. D. Steel, G. L. Reckitt, (the brother of Maurice) D. L. G. Joseph, who had peaked a year before in a spectacular victory in the final of the Open Championship against D. D. Steel and Col. C. E. Wilson, a determined, though less distinguished player who nonetheless helped his side to beat the visitors by six games to nil, a pattern which, unfortunately for the Australians, was continued throughout their visit.

But no sooner had the losers arrived home than they issued a challenge to play another international – this time in Australia. The main problem that this presented for the English team was financial. The Council cast about for funds, hampered by the fact that raising a subscription to send a team would contravene the players' amateur status, a question of 'professionalism' which still returns to haunt croquet (see chapter ten). However, a solution was found in the form of Sir Francis Colchester-Wemyss, later President of the Croquet Association who, as a passionate supporter of the game, volunteered himself as benefactor and organizer and cheerfully took up the tactful invitation to become captain.

Three Test matches were played, England won the first, lost the second and drew the third so that the series was decided upon games which left Australia the victor by twenty to nineteen. Following this tour, a short visit was made to New Zealand where an unofficial Test was played. This set the scene for a triangular contest.

Great Britain did not participate in the first Test between Australia and New Zealand in 1930. The distance was too far and the cost too great for another tour so soon after the last but in 1935, the first triangular Test took place when England and New Zealand played in Australia. International croquet had finally taken hold and Test matches between the three countries are now an established feature.

In Australia the 'tyranny of distance' has hindered the national organization of the game and all has not been resolved by the formation of the Australian Croquet Association. The ACA is unique in that it is an affiliation of individual state bodies each of which retains its own sovereignty. Each state elects two delegates to the ACA and they in turn make up the Council. Mindful of the independence of the state they represent, the delegates do not always act in favour of a nationwide policy. Interstate rivalries have caused clashes which sometimes result in a less than united Australian front, a fact which has much to do with the great distances between states' capital cities and the problems of staging interstate competitions. Partly because of this, there is no national ranking system but the National Championships, held annually in a different state capital, brings top players together.

This event, the highlight of the Australian croquet year, is a three-week-long carnival which in addition to play, provides an opportunity for the annual meeting of the national Council and of various committees concerned with regulating the game. Traditionally, play starts with an interstate competition for the Eire Cup, won from Ireland at the Carrickmines Club in Dublin in 1937. In 1949, the Australian Croquet Council was formed to administer the event.

South Australia has dominated the interstate championships for the last twenty or so years. A mediterranean climate (and legendary coaching at Brighton Croquet Club), produces players who soon reach top level and can practise throughout the year. The dry weather is hard on lawns and makes maintenance an expensive business which in turn affects club finances. Almost half the clubs are in metropolitan areas. Those in the country are separated by long distances which can make 'friendly' interclub matches nearly impossible. This is particularly so in Western Australia where some 650 croquet players are spread between thirteen metropolitan clubs in Perth and thirteen country clubs. One of these clubs, in the old mining town of Kalgoorlie, situated 600 kilometres east of Perth, dates back to 1939.

Each state has its own competitions and its own approach to the game. New South Wales has introduced a computer-based handicapping system which moves players' handicaps up and down to indicate present form. Canberra, the seat of Australian government, hosts two major croquet tournaments each year, one at Easter and the other on Australia Day. In the south eastern mainland state of Victoria, an annual treat is the Harry Gleeson twisted mallet event. It is held in the former gold-mining town of Maldon and contestants use a mallet with a twisted shaft which looks about as malleable as one of Alice's flamingos.

Until the outbreak of the First World War, the majority of Australian croquet players were men. Bowls was extremely popular at this time and as clubs and bars were restricted to men only, women took over the croquet scene. Today, nine tenths of Australian croquet players are women, many of them in the middle to older age group. Few however, make it to the top of the league. Here, one of Australia's developing players is a twenty-one-year-old (born in 1968) called Greg Bury from Bundaberg north of Brisbane. He started playing croquet at the age of twelve and went on to receive tuition from Bruce Fleming, one of Brisbane's top players. A steady young man with an agreeable temperament (all-important in croquet), he plays with a small-headed mallet and is known for his hard hitting. Like most of the Australian players (and also the New Zealanders), he concentrates on every shot and is reported to be able to pick up a break from thin air.

New Zealand

As in Australia, croquet appears to have been introduced to the country by settlers in the 1850s whose personal baggage often contained a boxed set of croquet equipment – a standard part of the paraphernalia of the Victorian middle-class family. It seems that the game was played on an organized basis as early as 1866 at Christchurch in the South Island but it was in the North Island, at Auckland, that the first official club was formed in 1879.

In 1910, the Canterbury Croquet Association was formed. Auckland soon followed suit and in 1913, the first New Zealand Championship tournament was played. It was won by Keith Izard, a New Zealander who had first made a stir in England while an undergraduate at Cambridge. Izard was renowned for his hard hitting and is even reputed to have broken the leg of a spectator who unwisely chose not to move out of his line of play.

War put an end to nationally organized events in New Zealand from 1916 to 1919 but in 1920, the New Zealand Croquet Council (NZCC) was formed and took over the national administration of the sport. Clubs developed and regional associations were formed. By the mid-Twenties, New Zealand was reported to have more players than England. Many of these were women, drawn into the game like their Australian counterparts, in reaction to the male-only atmosphere of bowls clubs. But one or two men players stood out, notably A. G. F. Ross, the first President of the NZCC.

Arthur Ross began his career by winning a doubles match in 1915. He had the distinction of beating D. D. Steel during the British team's unofficial tour of New Zealand and captained the New Zealand teams in the 1950 and 1956 Tests. He was New Zealand Champion at least eleven times and British Open Champion in 1954. His writings on croquet include the *Croquet Handbook*, first published in New Zealand in 1957, a comprehensive work 'entirely concerned with the technical details of croquet'. As such it was definitely not designed for the general reader.

The 1950 series against Great Britain was played in Auckland, Wellington and Dunedin. New Zealand won by two to one with Arthur Ross and his son-in-law, Ashley Heenan, forming a formidable doubles pair who twice beat British players H. O. Hicks and D. J. V. Hamilton-Miller. Former British Champion John Solomon also played in this Test and his memories are chiefly of food – 'copious quantities' of cream cakes, pavlovas and brandy snaps.

It seems that large crowds of spectators turned out to watch the series which crowned croquet's popularity in New Zealand. But it was short-lived. By the time the next team had returned from England in defeat in 1956, club membership had begun to drop. In twenty years, it fell by around 2,000 to settle near the 4,000 level. This decline was not helped by the sudden rise in popularity of women's bowls which changed the balance in many of the clubs, where croquet had always been associated with bowls – as the ladies' alternative to the men's game. It was the old story of merger and takeover which characterized the relationship between tennis and croquet in England at the start of this century.

The loss was keener because some of the New Zealand ladies had now achieved top level status. Principal among them was Mrs Clem Watkins (her husband was a Test player whose career coincided with that of Arthur Ross). She won the New Zealand Open Championship four times and the Women's Open Championship seven times. The 1950 Test team included two lady players – Miss M. Claughton (later Mrs I. H. Ashton) and Mrs W. H. Kirk who played again in the 1956 Test alongside Miss I. Wainwright, Mrs G. McKenzie-Smart and Clem Watkins. (Unfortunately, the latter suffered a heart attack in the second Test and was unable to continue play). On both occasions, the English team contained only one woman.

During the Sixties, New Zealand unsuccessfully contested two triangular Tests, one at home (1963), the other away in Australia (1969) but the low-point was brightened in 1963 by the first appearance of John Prince, who at seventeen years of age was the youngest player ever to appear in the MacRobertson Shield. Prince belonged to the croquet dynasty started by E. J. Ross, one of the founders of the New Zealand Croquet Council. His son Arthur, as already mentioned, coached Ashley Heenan (currently President of the World Croquet Federation) who in turn introduced John Prince to the game. Prince was the first of a series of players who have since taken the New Zealand game to a higher level. A bank official from Lower Hutt near Wellington, he has won some forty or so major national titles and has represented New Zealand in seven Test series. He ascribes much of his success to practice and reflects that the biggest change in New Zealand croquet is the increased numbers of men in tournament play. True, much of the croquet in the 120 clubs throughout New Zealand, is still played by women, especially in small towns and rural areas but at top level, only Madeline Hadwin now holds her own against the men who began to take command of New Zealand croquet in the Seventies.

In 1974, the first all-male team arrived in England for the triangular Test. Robert Jackson, an international table tennis player, who took up croquet in 1971 when he was nearing forty, made his first Test appearance. (He later went on to become one of New Zealand's Big Four and now manufactures mallets as well as taking part in the game.) John Prince won nine of his twelve games but Great Britain beat New Zealand three-nil. In the next Test in New Zealand however, the home side reversed the score and beat Great Britain (and also Australia) by three-nil. This clean sweep of a Test series (Great Britain had little excuse as it fielded a strong side) heralded the arrival of two more young players both still in their teens: Paul Skinley and Joe Hogan.

Paul Skinley is part Maori and has an elegant though slightly extraordinary style which includes doing a peculiar stamping foot movement before striking the ball. The colourful head and wrist bands he wears seem to belong more to the world of tennis than the croquet scene but with three New Zealand Championships and several Tests behind him, Skinley has established himself as a leading international player. He uses the Solomon grip and his concentration and deliberation make him a fascinating player to watch. Less stylish perhaps, but a definite master of the art is Joe Hogan.

In 1986, Hogan stunned croquet aficionados at Hurlingham with a virtuoso display in the British Opens. He met British Champion Nigel Aspinall in the semi-finals and the two played a magnificent match. Hogan took the first game by two points. In the second, he pegged out Aspinall's forward ball, leaving himself a lead of seven points but Aspinall proceeded to demonstrate the perfect way to win a two-ball game. The third game saw Aspinall ahead, leaving Hogan with a challenge which he met like a champion going on to take the game and the match with a flourish.

The final was an all-New Zealand affair as Hogan met Jackson. Hogan won in straight games, leaving Martin Murray, former chairman of the Croquet Association, to conclude in his report in the gazette, 'If anyone is entitled to call himself World Champion, it must be Joe Hogan.'

In 1989, Hogan dismissed any remaining doubt by returning to Hurlingham to win the first World Singles Championship. He is a cheerful character whose most singular characteristic is his relentless control of his game. A trained carpenter who also studied for a career in the priesthood, Joe Hogan is a great exponent of adopting the 'right psychology'. Like most of the New Zealand players, this seems to mainly consist of an undemonstrative but unyielding determination to win. During the late Seventies and Eighties, Hogan, Skinley, Prince and Jackson dominated the New Zealand croquet scene. Beginning with Jackson in 1975, one of these four 'musketeers' has, to date, won the New Zealand Open Championships and in recent years, Jackson and Hogan have also dominated the Doubles Championship.

The consistency of their play is remarkable. All four took part in the World Singles Championships in 1989 and they gave a collective lesson in croquet as a precise and professional game which at top level, requires far more than average skill.

The United States

In 1985, a British commentator wrote that it would be 'many years' before the Americans could boast 'the "strength in depth" of the MacRobertson Shield nations'. Five years later they have already made great strides towards this goal and in the meantime, have invested croquet with an enthusiasm which has been sadly lacking in the British game. In the mid-Eighties the Americans were at the front of a small revolution in croquet, especially on the question of professionalism (see chapter ten). It remains to be seen how much of this will eventually rub off onto the British game.

Croquet has been played in America since the mid-nineteenth century. Arthur Lillie wrote 'the first attempt at scientific croquet in that country came from Wimbledon'. This was in a set of conference laws reprinted in America in 1878. Lillie went on to quote the 1897 rules thus: 'Meetings of the leading players were held in 1880 and 1881 in New Ipswich, New Hampshire, where two fine courts were built by the home club.'

The National American Croquet Association, incorporating twenty-five local clubs, was founded in 1882 during a convention held at the New York Croquet Club on 127th Street and 5th Avenue but an American interest in croquet already existed in the 1860s, largely encouraged by immigrant travellers. Winslow Homer painted a series of idyllic portraits of croquet and several books appeared on the subject. Then, as now, American croquet was rather different to the British game. 'The Americans have their own croquet terminology,' wrote Lillie. 'An all-round break is "running the field", wiring is "tying up", laying a break is "setting up". The "dead ball" does not mean, as with us, the adversary's non-player (which in America is called the "innocent ball"); it means a ball already roqueted. The "guilty ball" is our "live ball".'

The 'garden game' also seems to have been played in rather different fashion. The habit of drinking between turns and gambling on the outcome of the match attracted displeasure among the more sober members of the community. The *New York Tribune* reported that a Boston clergyman had denounced the 'skirring and whirring of innocuous balls over the greensward as "dangerous, demoralising and sinful"' and a late-nineteenth century edition of the magazine *The Living Age* claimed that nothing was 'better calculated to bring out all the evil passions of humanity than the so-called game of croquet'.

However, croquet's greatest enemy was tennis and when the smart set dropped it, the game was relegated to the 'backyard'. Here it continued to use a nine hoop (or 'wicket' as it is called in the States) and two peg setting that had been abandoned in England in 1872.

During the Twenties, croquet re-emerged in American society when it was taken up by the literati and Hollywood. Columnist and critic Alexander Woollcott and the first winner of the Pulitzer prize for journalism, Herbert Bayard Swope, reintroduced the game to the East coast Smart Set while movie moguls Darryl Zanuck and Samuel Goldwyn became its leading exponents on the West Coast. Harpo Marx, George Saunders, Tyrone Power and Louis Jourdan were among the early stars of the greenswards but when Goldwyn became ill, the water was turned off at the two championship level lawns at his Beverly Hills home and by the Fifties, the game was once again in the 'backyard', played with rubber mallets (like those so strongly advocated by Arthur Lillie) and undersized balls. Here it remained until the Sixties.

In 1966, the Westhampton Mallet Club from Long Island challenged a British team and were soundly beaten at the Hurlingham Club. The next year, a British team saw for themselves the problems of the American game when they visited Long Island and were confronted with the nine-wicket and two-peg setting and lawns badly in need of a shave. Describing the occasion in a special Croquet Association supplement entitled 'Hurlingham Goes West', one of the visiting players, Douglas Strachen observed 'the grass is long – about an inch. We estimated that you have to hit a ball about five times as hard as on an English surface to make it travel the same distance.'

Fortunately for croquet, a figure emerged who provided America's answer to Walter Jones Whitmore. This was Jack Randall Osborn, an industrial designer, born in San Francisco, whose varied career before he discovered croquet had also included a brief period as an advertising salesman and a television producer. A founding member of the Westhampton Mallet Club in Long Island, Osborn was able to observe the English game at first hand when he played at Hurlingham in 1968. He had formed the New York Croquet Club, went on to help internationalize the American game and created a national croquet body. His efforts were rewarded in 1977 with the formation of the United States Croquet Association. Osborn became the first President of the USCA, a job which he held until 1989 when he finally stepped down in favour of Foxy Carter. His contribution to the sport has been variously described as 'immense' and 'legendary'. He is more modest. In the book he co-authored with Jesse Kornbluth *Winning Croquet – from Backyard to Greensward* (1983) he states that though the USCA's aims were 'ultimately as large as Walter Jones Whitmore's had been', the initial goal was to get together enough clubs to hold a national tournment. Some of those that came forward appear to have been delightfully unlikely. One played its matches on the twelfth floor of a bank building, another consisted of a single family, a third, the Alaska Croquet Club of Anchorage claimed the shortest croquet season in the world with most games taking place between 3.30 a.m. and 11.30 p.m. in the single month of June.

The diversities in the game were reconciled by a unified set of laws for two standard games. The nine-wicket and two-peg setting, in use for over eighty years, was retained while a six-wicket game was introduced, using the English setting but keeping some of the old laws, notably that of playing the colours in 'sequence'.

In 1977 when the United States Croquet Association (USCA) was formed, there were five clubs in America. By 1990 there were well over 200. Throughout the Eighties, the game enjoyed a startling revival, at one stage boasting position as the third fastest growing sport after surfing and volleyball. Professional coach Ted Prentis of Palm Beach, conducted 'coaching safaris' across the country. Books and videos provided additional self-teaching aids. Attractive prizes and glossy social events also lured new people to the game but status and style often outdistanced real skill on the lawns. However, in recent years the American players have taken a keener interest in events played to international association rules. British players have visited the prestigious Palm Beach Club in Florida where beautiful lawns and beautiful people make croquet an elegant and elitist game.

In 1986, a Californian vineyard proprietor invited players from New Zealand, Australia, and Great Britain to join the US players in an international singles event at Sonoma-Cutrer. It was won by British player Stephen Mulliner (who also won it for the next two years) with the highest placed American lying in thirteenth position. What the Americans lacked in croquet skill on this occasion, they more than made up for with the graciousness of their hospitality with cooked breakfasts served at the winery each morning before play commenced and large terraces with tables, chairs and sun umbrellas overlooking the lawns. Wrote one player, 'At five o'clock every evening a group of mallard ducks in single file went past the lawns returning about an hour later. They always followed the same route.'

In 1989, the USA, sent representatives to the official World Championships at Hurlingham. Jerry Stark, a blonde giant from Phoenix, Arizona, made a particular impression. Not so much for his play, learned in traditional 'backyard' style – interspersing turns at the game by consuming the contents of a crate of beer, (though he proved his worth in at least one game where he startled spectators with a sensational peg out from the fourth corner) – but for his likeable, friendly nature. He won the 'Fun Cup', donated by the Italians, in recognition of his geniality and his trendsetting sartorial contribution of flat cap, a unique version of plus fours and red braces.

The element of dressing – whether 'up' or 'down' (or a combination of both, players at gala events in Palm Beach wear 'Black Tie' and sneakers) and 'fun' in American croquet – is often sadly lacking in the contemporary British game, not least because of financial considerations. An advertisement in the first US *Croquet Gazette* (started by Osborn) announced 'a Croquet Ball with "Champagne and Croquet" followed by "the Croquet Ball" at the Tavern on the Green'. This was to include cocktails, dinner (crabmeat mousse stuffed with baby shrimp and chunks of avocado, contrefilet of beef with Perigourdine Sauce) dancing and guest croquet games, 'including Shoot the Sticky Wickets for valuable prizes'. American croquet under the USCA is run much more like a business operation. The USCA controls sales of equipment and markets a wide range of 'croquet merchandise', from T-shirts to car stickers. Croquet in America receives no government or local authority subsidy so the USCA relies on events to help pull in finance. In 1984, the first Celebrity Event at the prestigious Florida Country Club collected considerable funds and more publicity from a single event than before or since. Such promotion requires a degree of style.

Walter Jones Whitmore would have approved. In 1871 he helped organize a tournament at Aldermaston at which bands played military music and 'spectators were four or five deep around the ground'. A second meeting at Aldershot received a lengthy report in a magazine of the period signed by a correspondent who called himself 'Rover' and who considered the event 'the most attractive tournament of the season. For besides the pretty club grounds with their numerous croquet lawns, large white marquees and colossal waving Union Jacks, besides Offenbach's music and the "crack" bands playing all day long (including one "monster" band, which was very successful), besides the large concourse of ladies and gentlemen, the gazers and the gazed at, there were many other non-croquet attractions, all crowded into this one week to make the meeting go off with as much éclat as possible.'

These included racing, cricket, two theatre performances in the club house of 'The Brigand' and 'Ici on parle Francais', an arranged fight and a march past when 17,000 men paraded under the command of the General of Division, Sir Hope Grant 'and last but not least, the Aldershot division on the Friday entertained the croquet strangers at a grand ball given at the clubhouse.'

In the spirit of 'entertainment' the Americans are well ahead in reviving croquet's more glamorous past but there are those who are increasingly concerned that the 'financial' element might take too strong a hold. 'Play for pay' has become a byword in American croquet and threatens to disrupt a season which is already crammed with events, beginning in Florida in January with the prestigious Palm Beach Invitational. The growth of the sport in America has continued at a cracking pace. In 1989, new clubs were joining the USCA at the rate of around ten a month, tournaments were expanding at the same hectic rate and croquet lawns were proliferating, whether at resorts (along with golf clubs), at universities, or in private homes. It remains to be seen whether or not this will ultimately, as some fear it might, change the traditional character of croquet.

Croquet Worldwide

Croquet is played in a surprising number of countries, from Canada (where its popularity increases annually) to the USSR and from Sweden to South Africa.

Colonialism and 'Empire' took the game to India. The July 1967 edition of the gazette carried on its cover a reproduction of an engraving showing girls playing croquet at the Lawrence Military Asylum near Simla around the year 1867. This establishment, situated at the foot of the Himalayas, offered a good climate and claimed to provide children of British soldiers in India with 'a plain, useful and religious education'.

The picture illustrates a swarm of young women playing croquet through vast hoops on rather poor grass. In 1897, Arthur Lillie wrote that croquet was 'quite a craze in India'. The Lieutenant-Governor of Bengal played and so did the Governor of the Central Provinces. A Surgeon-General wrote to Lillie saying that he believed the game had been introduced to Simla in 1864 as he found it popular there 'when I first played it at Simla in the spring of 1865. During that season and up

31

to the end of 1870, the game was in full swing at Simla, and it was also played more or less at every station from Peshawar to Calcutta.'

Lillie's correspondent, J. T. C. Ross, went on to write, 'I have a photograph of croquet players at Simla in 1865 in which mallets are seen mostly with small heads, such as at first came from England with the regular set of those days; but as knowledge of the game progressed and the courts got larger, heavier mallets were made locally. They used the Rouse – the Simla mountain ash – for handles, and lignum vitae and wild boxwood for the head. The viceroy played with an entire ivory mallet, handle and all – as became his position – and as in the present day, there was no restriction in size or shape.'

Gradually, it seems, the game fell from favour. Badminton and Lawn Tennis took over and long before the last days of the Raj, popular sports included riding, shooting, polo and pig-sticking with violent bouts of tennis and later squash, being played by the ladies.

Croquet had reached Ceylon by 1898 and the Ceylon Golf, Tennis and Croquet Championships took place every February. An elderly contributor to the gazette recalled in 1970 that at the end of the nineteenth century, croquet in Ceylon 'had taken a new lease of life. The lawn had boundaries: no longer could one knock one's opponent to the far end of the garden, or into a bush if possible. The hoops were made narrower, and the cage in the middle of the ground with a bell suspended inside had been banished.' (This odd piece of equipment does not appear much in the English history of the game. According to Lillie, it was largely confined to a version of the game played at Eglinton Castle and Cassiobury Park in Essex – along with the fashion of wearing red boots.) In 1905, the membership of the club stood at about 200.

Croquet still retains a stronghold in South Africa where the game has been played since 1860. In 1936 the South African Croquet Association was formed and membership currently includes some eleven clubs of which Rondebosch in Cape Town, is probably the largest.

There have always been close links between the UK Croquet Association and South African croquet. This co-operation, unacceptable to some members of the CA, has been fostered by the fact that several British champions migrated to South Africa. Notable amongst these was Edward Ward Petley who had taken part in the 1935 and 1950 Tests. He had twice partnered Miss D. D. Steel to victory in the Mixed Doubles and when interviewed on the subject in South Africa in

1983 said, 'She told me exactly what to do and I did it.' Another British born player is Leslie Riggall, an economist and horticulturist and also an expert on the American game who, in the mid-Eighties, conducted a lengthy correspondence with British player Keith Aiton in the pages of the gazette on the subject of TPOs (triple peels on opponent). Aiton, with resort to a certain amount of formal logic, argued in favour of the tactic. Riggall objected that the TPO was overrated as simply 'bold and spectacular play'. The correspondence thundered on between Nottingham, England and Kloof, South Africa and finally ended in honourable compromise.

In recent years, South Africa has produced some exceptional players. Notably Tom Barlow, a farmer from Somerset West Croquet Club, who dominated the South African championships for a decade, beginning in the early Seventies, and was runner up in the British Opens in 1975 and Reginald Bamford, still in his twenties who, at fourteen was already ranked sixth in his country.

The subject of South Africa's participation in the World Championships in 1989 came up for debate at the same time as the continued Croquet Association policy of presenting 'medals' to overseas associations including South Africa. With typical overreaction, questions flew back and forth between Council and the CA membership and also included the Sports Council and New Zealand. The NZCC made it clear that participation by South African players would necessitate a boycott by New Zealand players. Panic ensued and South Africa was excluded from the World Championships though not barred from participation in all CA events as some had hoped. Instead, a compromise agreement was adopted which stated 'the CA's abhorrence of apartheid', declared its support for non-racial sport and 'enshrined in policy' the fact that competitors in CA events were regarded as sharing those attitudes. It was a triumph of diplomacy for all concerned. The CA could still lay claim to its moral virtue and South African players had been saved from a total ban.

Meanwhile South Africa continued to play croquet. In the early Eighties, the basic laws of the game were translated into Afrikaans. The translation was taken from Professor Bernard Neal's condensed version of the full laws and it was decided to forgo the Dutch derivation 'Kroukie' for an internationally accepted word (as is the case with 'rugby') and the association opted for the title 'Suid Afrikaanse Croquet Vereniging'.

In North Africa, croquet remains popular in Egypt, especially in the Cairo area. Most notable of the Cairo clubs is the splendid Gazira Club situated on an island in the middle of the Nile. Lt.-Col. Denis Brown, currently a member of Compton Club in East Sussex, recalls taking up croquet there during the war. 'It was in 1941. We were walking through the Gazira Club one day, myself and another fellow and we saw these two croquet lawns. I'm told they were flooded with the Nile water and they were absolutely like a billiard table. I've never seen a court like it, or such perfect surroundings. Anyhow, this chap came down on the court and said "Have you ever played this game?" So we said "No" and he said "Would you like to know something about it?" and thereupon he took us in hand.'

They were lucky for the 'chap' in question was Major Robert Tingey, one of the great players of the Thirties, a 'notable tactician' and an authorized coach for the Croquet Association. Lt.-Col. Brown recalls that Tingey had also trained one of the local ball boys at the Gazira club into a first-class croquet player. Tingey won the Men's Championship in 1939 and later retired to live in Australia where he was instrumental in the formation of the Australian Croquet Association. His Australian wife, Clare, died in 1971 after which Tingey did not return to England. He died in 1978.

Croquet has been played in such contrasting surroundings as Norway and Northern Thailand. The British Consulate-General in the town of Chiangmai once provided a beautiful setting for a full-size lawn beside the river that runs through Thailand's northern capital. Two gardeners spent their days heaving a full-size roller back and forth across the grass which was watered regularly and surrounded by flowerbeds. Play usually began in the late afternoon and at six o'clock promptly, a servant would appear at the edge of the lawn to take orders for drinks. Unfortunately, the Consulate building and therefore the lawn, no longer belongs to the British government. However, the diplomatic service seems to have played its part in keeping croquet alive in other outposts. A letter to the Summer 1978 gazette refers to play amongst the diplomatic corps in Nigeria. One of the keenest partipants was the then Minister of the British High Commission, Mr J. R. Williams who, it seems, had also taken his croquet set 'en poste' through India, Indonesia and the Fiji Islands.

Croquet on the Continent is currently in a state of revival, with the Italians and French both expressing interest in the game. In France, official croquet almost disappeared though during the Seventies, it was apparently played on the sands of St Malo in Brittany, where an official document of May 1974 stated, *'Association malouine de croquet Union-Libre. Objet: favoriser et exercer la practique du croquet et susciter des liens d'amitie entre ses membres'*. In an odd contradiction, the game in France is considered an 'English' sport. Apparently, it was thought to be so as long ago as Arthur Lillie's day for he writes that the *Figaro* newspaper had published a summer number with illustration of polo, Lawn Tennis and other 'English games' which included croquet, called 'crockett'. French rules it seems, were different to the English and involved a degree of gallic subtlety which, according to Lillie, excluded 'all that does not suit French conditions'.

Lillie himself observed croquet being played in northern France and his description of the occasion is quite idyllic.

'Three years ago,' (that was, sometime around 1894), 'I found myself at a modest little seaport in Brittany. The hotel, primitive but comfortable, was separated by the road from an enclosure which contained a *"pavilion"* where we drank our coffee after dinner. The sea washed the wall at high tide.

'This enclosure was spread with fine gravel, amongst which were croquet hoops . . . all day long the hoops were occupied.'

Countries which still boast active croquet clubs include Jamaica, Mexico, Portugal, Switzerland, Tenerife and Spain. There are also claims that the game is played in China and even in the USSR. The story goes that Averill Harriman, a notably keen croquet player, insisted that a croquet lawn be set up at the American Embassy in Moscow during his time there as ambassador. A contributor to the *New Zealand Croquet Gazette* also asserted that Russian cosmonauts were made to play croquet to help reorientate them on their return to earth and went on from this to speculate on whether the game could thus help 'depression and other related illnesses' in New Zealand.

Croquet is also increasingly popular in Japan where it has made rapid progress.

The Japanese game of 'Gate Ball' which first became popular after the Second World War, has some features of croquet in that it also uses mallets, balls and hoops. It is played on a lawn a little less than a half size croquet lawn and involves the use of golf strokes and a great deal of energy. In 1982, a Japanese Professor of Sport Sociology who had made a study of Gate Ball and found that its origins derived from the

American nine-wicket two-peg 'backyard setting', visited the USA and England. His enthusiasm stimulated Japanese interest in the six-peg setting. In 1983, the Croquet Association of Japan was formed, British Association laws were adopted and the first National Championship took place a year later. An Australian player who had written to the CAJ expressing his interest in croquet in Japan, found himself taking part. Writing about the occasion in *The Australian Croquet Gazette* he noted that the event took place in November in Odawara, a small town near the sea, on three-quarter size courts planted with artificial turf. The game began with the 'stones, scissors or paper' game, the usual way to 'toss a coin' in Japan.

In 1983, Professor Bernard Neal of the Croquet Council was invited on a coaching trip to Japan where he and Teddy Prentis of the USA gave demonstrations. Japan in turn sent a small contingent to England to watch Great Britain play Australia in the Test match at Colchester in 1986. Three years later Japan sent another team, including their champion Toru Takano who participated in the World Championship. On this occasion, Takano came up against the formidable figure of British player Richard Hilditch and failed to get beyond the first round. However, in an astonishingly short period of time, most certainly in croquet terms, the Japanese game has developed at a great rate and their international debut was most creditable.

Scotland, Ireland and Wales

Both Scotland and Ireland have made their individual contribution to the history of the game and all three nations have produced players for internationals played by Great Britain. Scottish croquet is believed to have started in Dumfriesshire in the 1870s. The early enthusiasts for the game were the ladies who seem to have exerted an elegant influence for in some clubs dances took place every evening and there were excursions during the afternoons. Arthur Lillie was impressed enough to make special mention of the elegant flowerbeds of one such club and its 'tasteful pavilion'. After the wars, the game was revived at an all-ladies club in Aberdeenshire.

Modern Association Croquet was not introduced to Scotland until 1950 with the founding of the Edinburgh Croquet Club, the first to join the Croquet Association. The Sixties saw a proliferation of clubs, enough to form the Scottish Croquet Committee in 1969 – under the guidance of the Croquet Association – with the aim of developing the game and inter-club friendly matches. The same year, the first official CA tournament was held in Scotland at Edinburgh. In 1974, Scotland formed its own Croquet Association (SCA) which has since received considerable help from the Scottish Sports Council and has attracted an interesting amount of sponsorship. A new national croquet centre has been established near Edinburgh and in 1989, it put in a strong bid to stage the 1990 World Singles Championships.

Ireland's contribution to croquet is unique. If only for the mass of speculation it has encouraged on the origins and the name of the game. One of the more entertaining summaries on the subject appeared in the June 1966 edition of the gazette. The authors wound their way from *Oxford Dictionary* to *Encyclopaedia Britannica* via several specialized texts to the conclusion that the word 'croquet' is a derivation of the gaelic *cluiche* meaning 'to play'. Be that as it may, the first Croquet Championship was played at Cork in 1861. It was won by a Mr Evans and the game gradually gained in popularity but then interest fell away.

In recent times, Ireland has at last begun to recover the force that it showed in croquet in its early years and during the Twenties. Though the country now has only one club with full-size lawns, Carrickmines, which is situated in a Dublin suburb, an Irish International Team, has taken part in US International Croquet Challenge Cup matches in Florida. Following this triumph the Croquet Association of Ireland (CAI) was formed in May 1985, affiliated to the parent organization in England. A year later there were already eight affiliated clubs. Among its top players Ireland boasts Colin Irwin, selected for the 1990 triangular Test in New Zealand, and John McCullough from County Donegal, who represented Great Britain in the 1986 series, is a top coach and has also co-authored an authoritative book on how to play the game.

Wales has only two small clubs and though it boasts a national team (which played against England at Colchester in 1982), in the main, the players belong to English clubs.

In 1986, England, Scotland, Ireland and Wales all fielded competitors for the Royal Bank Nations Trophy. The significance of this particular occasion was that it marked croquet's first televized broadcast. Granada filmed the event in Manchester but for one reason or another it proved to be of limited success and 'viewer impact' was muted (see chapter 10).

There is little doubt that competitive croquet is gaining interest worldwide. In 1989, the World Croquet Federation included in its objectives the aims of holding world team championships, of representing croquet at the World Games and of obtaining sponsorship and government funding for the game. In principle, such ambitions are very laudable but there are those who wonder if so much change can be brought to the game without fundamentally altering its character. However, croquet's 'character' is largely formed by the people who have, and still do, play the game and so far, each generation has produced its fair share of eccentrics, both male and female.

THE LADIES' GAME

There are remarkably few females who survive at the top of croquet today, yet women have had a considerable part to play in the development of the game and it was their wholehearted enthusiasm for croquet which first made it popular. The Victorian picture of a young lady standing with her foot on a ball, about to take 'tight' croquet that first appeared in 1862, has been reproduced on many occasions (examples hang in the clubhouses at Southwick and at Roehampton) and reappeared on the front of the gazette in July 1967. The plump young woman in question wears a voluminous hooped skirt and a silly little tricorn hat with a feather. She is about to swing a small mallet and is staring in doe-eyed fashion at a young man who fingers his moustache nervously. Under the title of the piece, 'A nice game for two or more', the caption says it all. 'Fixing her eyes on his and placing her pretty little foot on the ball, she said "Now, then, I am going to Croquet you!" and Croquet'd he was completely.'

No doubt a degree of flirtation did go on during these games but one wonders if it was really any more than that which Jane Austen had described some fifty years earlier. A game of croquet was not the first occasion for a young woman of those times to escape the beady eye of her chaperone. What it did provide, was the novelty of a game played in the open air which required the same degree of skill from both sexes and which could be enjoyed by all ages. If only for these reasons, it was bound to be popular at the country house parties that characterized the leisured life of the time.

The cheating and trickery that occurred during this early garden croquet was, as it is today, all part of the enjoyment. In *Croquet* published in 1899, Leonard B. Williams describes how 'In the old garden party days it was considered very good fun to move your ball to a more favourable position, and to commit other peccadilloes of a similar nature. However, croquet was not then a scientific game. Instead of being the billiards, chess, or whist of the lawn and the open air, it more nearly resembled the 'grab' or 'beggar-my-neighbour' with which we were familiar in our nursery days, and the ethics of these games were carefully observed at garden parties and similar entertainments.' In her *Manners for Women*, published two years before Mr Williams' book, the then oracle on social behaviour, Mrs Humphreys, or 'Madge' as she was also known, gave a rather alarming view of the life of the poor hostess at these country house gatherings.

'Unless she chances to be a woman possessing some force of character, her good nature is taken advantage of, and she is induced to send out invitations to friends of her guests, unknown to herself, and the results are sometimes far from pleasant. The fast and furious fun that goes on at some of these country house parties may be in the highest degree disagreeable to her, but, having given the invitations to the persons who originate and enjoy the practical joke form of pastime, she is helpless and powerless during the remainder of their stay.'

Small wonder if she took refuge in encouraging them to take their high spirits away to the croquet lawn for as long as possible.

The days of 'tight' croquet (i.e. playing a croquet shot with a foot on one ball) obviously had their drawbacks. Leonard Williams describes that 'It was by no means unusual to see a player, generally a lady, in endeavouring to execute this stroke miss the ball altogether, bringing her mallet with an audible whack into contact with her ankle. She would then drop the mallet and spin round the lawn in an agony of pain and lamentation.'

Not surprisingly perhaps the ladies began to lose interest. The most usual explanation is that as croquet grew more formalized they became discouraged and they complained about the increasing complexity of new rules. However, it seems more likely that the garden players were gradually seduced by other novelties, such as cycling, which merited a separate section for dress and comportment in Mrs Humphreys' book in 1897 (and in which croquet is not mentioned at all). Cycling was certainly much more fun for women like Gwen Raverat and her intrepid mother. In her delightful book, *Period Piece*, Miss Raverat recalled how they played 'the classic games' but were not good at them; 'On the whole, we thought them rather dull'. So they invented new games of their own, including 'Tennicroque, in which you had to move croquet balls about by throwing tennis balls at them'. Cycling proved much more fun, though rather dangerous for she recalls seeing 'the most appalling cuts and bruises' on her mother's legs as the result of frequent tumbles.

Luckily for croquet, some young women still found the game far from dull. A few of the earliest tournaments were grand social affairs. At Aldershot, for example, it was 'simply perfection' as the entertainment might also include a ball where a girl could hope to find an almost inexhaustible selection of dancing partners, 'golden horse artillerymen, sombre riflemen, red dragoon guards, linesmen skilled in the spring waltz and light cavalry efficient in the galop'.

One such event was dominated by the 'brilliant play of a very young lady, Miss E. A. Helme'. She completely bowled over one of her audience who recorded her triumph with great gusto and obvious appreciation, saying that she 'exhibited an accuracy of eye and hand, combined with a judgement "pluck" and power of mallet which bids fair to make her a facile conqueror in future ladies meetings. On one occasion she made both her balls rovers (the final hoop) in twelve minutes, picking up the break by a splendid shot through a hoop at eight yards, and carrying her first ball round before the four balls were in the game and her second ball the ensuing turn. If a treacherous hole near the stick had not prevented her from pegging out, she would have finished the shortest game on record.' Her triumphs seem to have ended here however for her name does not appear in the record books. Others arrived to win the Women's Championship including Miss Walter and Mrs Walsh and Miss Maud Drummond. The latter was an attractive girl who learnt her game on her father's lawns at Petworth. She won the title of Gold Medallist in 1896 and was Ladies Open Champion in 1897.

According to Leonard Williams she was 'one of the most brilliant, and quite the most successful player of the day'. Another was Miss Maud de Winton (sometimes spelt de Winta), gold medallist in 1897, who looks a rather stern character in the portrait which appears in Williams' book. Both ladies played 'side-style'. The long dresses of the period would have made it difficult for them to do anything else.

The first ladies' championship was played at Bushey Hall in Hertfordshire in 1869.

'Tight' croquet was banned which raised some protests. However, the tournament was won by a Mrs Joad who was presented with a necklace. Little else is known of her. She never won again, nor did her husband, who became the first Croquet Champion of England in the same year. He was described in the gazette as a 'leading player' at Worthing and other Sussex clubs and one of those who encouraged 'the muscular element' in the game and also favoured smaller hoops with greater distances between them. In 1870, the first Ladies' Championship to be played at Wimbledon was won by Miss Walter, using the one-handed style. Most of the top ladies of the period seem to have been introduced to the game gradually, either by their families, or their husbands but one young woman whose name is now synonymous with croquet, appeared quite suddenly, as if from nowhere.

As a young girl, Lily Gower was a beauty. Slim, small-waisted, with a luxurious head of hair, a rather intense expression in her eyes and possessing slender hands with long fingers. She was described as tall 'with a fine head of golden hair' and contemporary photographs show her as an elegant young creature. Perhaps her grandest portrait is reproduced in Prichard's book where she appears posing for the camera in full Edwardian finery, complete with preposterous hat. For play, she seems to have adopted a less extravagant style, wearing a small straw boater and a simple blouse and skirt. She played with a long-handled mallet (weighing three pounds) which she held right at the very top of the shaft with one hand, the other placed twelve inches or so lower down, index finger pointing straight down the shaft, in much the same style as Joe Hogan, winner of the first World Championships, does today. Some forty or so years later, Lily was photographed, still holding her mallet in exactly the same way though by then she had lost her slender figure and looked a portly creature, crowned by an unattractive cloche hat.

From the start, Lily Gower caused a stir. Her striking appearance and the fact that she walked straight into a tournament at Budleigh Salterton in 1898 to beat the reigning champion (C. E. Willis), set the croquet world alight. Arthur Lillie gave a description of her debut which captures the excitement of the occasion.

'A strange rumour was carried to players still involved in matches on distant lawns. The novice was playing very well and was running rapidly ahead of her formidable opponent. Soon, so it was reported, a ringing cheer startled the quiet town of Budleigh Salterton. Miss Gower, the novice, had won the first game. As can be imagined, the interest was now enormous. All the spectators and every contestant not actually playing a game, gathered round the lawn. Every stroke of the game was watched with breathless interest. Mr Willis produced some of his finest play and won easily. Again the habitual commentators were in evidence with such remarks as "She was lucky in the first game but experience tells in the end". They were, however, completely confounded because in the third game Mr Willis had only five shots. Lily went round in two breaks of eleven points and twelve points and won by twenty-six points in thirty-five minutes.'

She continued her success later in the year by winning at Wimbledon (the Maidstone Club had requested the All England Lawn Tennis and Croquet Club to permit their usual competitions to be played there because of an outbreak of typhoid). Two Cups were to be contested, the Ladies Challenge Cup held by Miss Lydia Elphinstone Stone (also known simply as 'Miss Stone') and the Open Challenge Cup in the possession of Mr Willis. Miss Gower entered both competitions. On Wednesday morning, wrote Lillie, she found herself confronting Miss Elphinstone Stone. 'The game fluctuated at first but Miss Gower was not very long in getting one ball round to the last hoop, assisted by one very forward and difficult break. Then with the other ball for the fourth hoop, she laid a trap for her opponent. Miss Stone fired, and her doom was sealed.' The next day, Lily met Mr Willis. By now, it seems, the players were suffering from 'tropical heat' but 'it was soon evident that this delicate young lady, although exhausted from having played several games in a hot sun, was a very formidable opponent. She pushed on, ball after ball with difficult breaks; she lost the innings three or four times and at once recovered it by amazing long shots. In the gloaming she pegged out having defeated the champion of the United All-England Association by twenty-one points.'

The *Ladies Field* described it as 'epoch-making' and 'the finest game of croquet ever played there'. She was then in her teens. Before this double triumph, she had never played on a full-size lawn before and had apparently learnt it all in a book. Lillie records that Miss Gower developed her game with her mother at Newcastle Emlyn in Wales.

'Miss Gower is very young, very delicate-looking. She stands quite upright to her stroke, and then takes aim by putting the mallet in the first instance over the ball. She then strikes with confidence, careless apparently, whether the object ball is six feet or six yards away. Her tactics are simple – to scheme for the four-ball break at all seasons. At this she is very deadly.'

She seems to have had a remarkable coolness. Leonard Williams describes how 'Nothing could exceed the apparent ease with which the most difficult strokes are accomplished, and after watching Miss Gower for some time, the spectator is tempted to enquire whether she has ever been known to break down.'

Lily certainly seemed to sweep all before her. *The Sportsman's Yearbook* looked back over her triumphant progress with suitable awe and at some length.

'The highest honours have been won by Miss L. Gower and Mr R. C. J. Beaton; but in that the lady has far oftener beaten this gentleman in individual matches, to Miss Gower must be conceded the first position.

'Miss Gower did not play at all in public until 20 June, when she entered for the Association Gold Medal with the gentlemen, as has been her custom since 1900. This she won without losing a single game in any of her six matches – twelve games. The following week she was again successful in the chief event in Hurlingham. But at Ranelagh, where she was not allowed to enter with the men, she succumbed to Miss Coote. For the Open Championship at Wimbledon she was most unexpectedly beaten in the first round by Mr F. Y. Horner, who was making a first appearance in a public tournament; but excuse may be made, for an extremely strong and gusty wind was blowing which made it difficult for her to stand in her usual poised position. The next week, however, she won the Champion Cup after a tie with Mr C. D. Locock. Miss Gower was also first in the Open Singles at Brighton and Reading, but at Eastbourne in a match of a single game she was again beaten by Miss Coote. Her success in Open Doubles has been proportionately as great for she won all she entered for – at Ranelagh with Mr DuCane, at Wimbledon with Mr Beaton and at Eastbourne with Mr Ackroyd. This is a complete record of this lady's performances in open events – truly a remarkable one.'

The edition of the Croquet Gazette for 29 June 1905 also paid its respects to Lily's year of triumph and tried to analyse the reason for her great success. 'Although Miss Gower has won practically every one of the other important events open to first-class players this is the first time on which we can have the pleasure of congratulating her on winning the highest prize in the croquet world, namely, the Championship of Croquet . . . Why does Miss Gower always win? Because she has more willpower and can control her nerves better than other players . . . She was playing from early morning till nearly seven o'clock, on an extremely hot day, taking part in six games, all of them exciting and her nerves came out of this ordeal in better condition than her opponents.'

Not everyone admired Miss Gower so openly. Her resounding success against the men that year earned her the displeasure of some of her own sex. One of them recalled much later that 'When she (Lily Gower) won the Open Championship and beat all the men it took some of the glory away from our Ladies' Championship.'

The same commentator remembered that Miss Gower, like all young ladies of the time, was chaperoned at tournaments. Even so, the young man she defeated so gloriously in 1905, obviously attracted her more than others for he soon became her husband. This was R. J. C. 'Reginald' Beaton, a strange looking fellow with a vast black beard who was chiefly distinguished by the consistency – for which some commentators substituted the word 'dull' – of his play. Together, the Beatons won the Doubles Championships two years in succession after their marriage, thereby becoming a famous croquet partnership which was later added to when one of their two sons also took up the game.

In his unpublished history of croquet, Maurice Reckitt recalled that 'Miss Gower was renowned for the steadiness of her break-making and the accuracy of her wiring . . . she was always a deliberate player, standing with her mallet poised above the ball for longer than most competitors are wont to do.'

Many years later, it was Reckitt who wrote her short obituary in the gazette. Her leading characteristics as a player, he noted, 'were her intense power of concentration and the pertinacity which won her success in many an uphill game.' In later years she appeared less skilful though she returned to win the Women's Championship in 1928 and won the Peel Memorials (for the third time) in 1948. She died in July 1959 at the age of eighty-two.

Lily Gower had her failings as a croquet player. Her style, as has already been remarked, lacked some of the dash and verve that characterized a few of her female contemporaries. But she earns her place in the croquet history books for the fact that delicate though she seemed, she had a will of iron and she used it intelligently to get to the very top of her game. No doubt in the process, she also helped to brush aside some of the cobwebs which had collected over Victorian women. The ladies may have been slightly shocked by her preference for playing against the opposite sex and even the men did not always like it. They voiced their discontent in grudging reports of her play but in the end, she won their respect as 'a shrewd tactician' – no mean praise in the croquet world. At the height of her triumph, Lily and her lady opponents were causing consternation amongst the men, one of whom wrote in the gazette, 'Croquet is the one outdoor game in which two sexes might be supposed to compete on equal terms. Activity is not required at all, physical force to a very slight extent, even a good eye is not really essential. Skirts, if properly managed are no drawback to most styles of play. Unsuitable hats are mere vanity. Nerve (as distinguished from "nerves"), manual skill and intelligence – these are the three requisites for success in tournament play. In which of these are the women deficient? Not, we think, in nerve.' The opposition was rattled.

The young woman who twice beat Lily Gower in 1904 was one of the Irish invasion referred to in chapter one. Nina Coote was a beautiful woman with large eyes and an aquiline nose and played with a rather wild vivacity that was in complete contrast to the more studied style of her closest rival. She won the Ladies' Open Championships in 1903 and again in 1905, the same year that she won the Mixed Doubles, the Irish Gold Medals, and the Gold Caskets. She played with the golfer's side-swing and usually completed her games in record time. *The Sportsman's Yearbook* of 1905 noted that 'Miss Coote seems very ambitious, entering for anything, but her all round form is curiously erratic and she is rather a puzzle to the handicapper'. Prichard also notes that Miss Coote was better known for her dash than her accuracy and has a rather odd tale to tell of how in later years, following a disappointment in love, she took up spiritualism and became convinced that she would die at the age of sixty-one, which she did. Her obituary in the gazette in 1945 makes no mention of this but reflects with melancholy, 'It seems so strange and so sad that such a vigorous personality has been taken from us.'

Another woman of this particular period worth special mention is Miss Olive Henry. Like Miss Coote and their contemporary May Chester, Miss Henry was a spirited player. She won the Ladies'

Championship and the Gold Medal in 1898. Leonard Williams, who grew quite lyrical about her accomplishment, wrote: 'Both these prizes were competed for in large and powerful fields, and on both occasions her pre-eminence was ungrudgingly conceded. The critic in the security of his sanctum might with some justice complain that her game is over-bold, but such is her execution, especially in long rushes that she compels admiration, even when her tactics are risky. No game in which she is engaged ever lacks incident or interest.' Small wonder that she was 'the lady whose play gave him most pleasure to witness'. One cannot help but speculate if it was simply Miss Henry's play that was so attractive for she was quite charming with a perfect hour-glass figure. Another female contemporary was moved to record of Miss Henry, 'I beat her once and all her young men admirers crowded round to console her. She was such a pretty creature.'

They make a lovely collection, these croquet ladies of the Edwardian period. Their long skirts with tightly-belted waists, high-collared blouses and jauntily-tilted hats are an elegant reflection of a graceful, leisured lifestyle. But their dress cannot have been easy to play in. One wonders how they did it, if the clothes were as constricting as Gwen Raverat would have us believe. She hated stays and wrote that except for the smallest-waisted 'naturally dumb-bell-shaped females, the ladies never seemed at ease'. Bodices wrinkled from strain and stays pushed and squeezed painfully. 'After the torture of stays came the torture of hats,' wrote Miss Raverat. She describes how uncomfortable in their precariousness were those giant confections of fruit and feathers. And indeed, some of the wilder examples worn for croquet portraits would appear to bear out her claim. Shoes also seem to have been a problem, for in 1870, 'Cavendish' (Henry Jones) of *The Field* complained against the practice of walking on turf in high-heeled boots. However, fashions were changing fast. Advertisements in the gazettes of the early 1900s offer more practical alternatives for the lady croquet player, including the 'Julie' showerproof games skirt ('folds into small compass, easily carried and slipped on in a moment') and all manner of garments made in 'Viyella'. 'With all the merits, and there are many, of the best flannel, Viyella is free from the disadvantages thereof as it never irritates the skin, actually improves with washing and is far less liable to shrinkage in the laundry'. Fashions had already changed considerably from the earliest days when Victorian ladies played in vast hooped skirts caught up by small chains, but by the time the next great player in the story of the ladies' game appears on the scene, the elegant frocks and frothy hats of the Edwardian era were also part of the past.

Dorothy Dyne Steel learnt to play at the Bedford Club (a famous spot for croquet in the Twenties which no longer exists), at the start of the century. Unlike Lily Gower, she did not appear suddenly but slowly worked her way to the top. Once there, she dominated the ladies' game, winning the Women's Championship an astonishing fifteen times (from 1932 to 1939 she took the title annually without a break). During a long career, and often in consecutive years, she won the Doubles Championship, the Mixed Doubles, the Open Championships, and the President's Cup (variously known until 1935 as the Champion Cup or the Beddow's Cup). No doubt she would have taken the Men's Gold Medal had women not been barred from entering the event in 1908. This decision had not been made without difficulty. There was considerable debate as to the 'fairness' of refusing the ladies entry and one letter to the gazette feared that the then Hon. Secretary of the CA would be forced 'to appear in full armour at the head of an indignant body of Amazons'. In fact, the decision finally passed off relatively peacefully. It was perhaps as well that it had been taken before the days of Miss Steel.

The Croquet Association possesses a large reproduction of a sepia tint photograph taken of Dorothy Dyne Steel in the Thirties. The great 'DD' stands surrounded by her many trophies like a burglar with his swag. She wears a mackintosh, tightly belted around her plump waist and with her squashed trilby hat and her steel-rimmed spectacles looks like the gestapo character in the popular BBC TV series 'Allo, Allo'. Her expression is quite awesomely determined.

'DD Steel' as she was best known, was the croquet world's equivalent of today's tougher tennis ladies. On court she was supremely accurate, playing with a precision characterized more by its force than its flair and dominating her opponent by her sheer determination to win. She was in her element in a crisis and never allowed her opponents to think they might beat her. The words 'pretty' or 'feminine' would not have suited her, for her progress through a game was less graceful than hypnotic. 'She moved at an absolutely even pace from the first stroke of her turns to the last,' wrote Maurice Reckitt who also thought she was 'probably the most infallible "machine for victory" in the history of the game'. She always played best under pressure and seems to have almost relished a reputation for being fierce, enjoying the supremacy she held in croquet and, according to Reckitt, delighted with the nickname accorded her of 'Stainless Steel'.

She made her presence felt in the croquet world both on and off the court. She was against the introduction of the 'lift' (the right to pick up the ball and play it from either baulk line) which was proposed by the Rev. Elvey in the Twenties, for she felt that it gave undeserved opportunity to players and she did not like the 'lengthening' of the game. She returned to the subject in 1955 in a correspondence with the then editor of the gazette.

'Why do games take so long – even among the best players? she wrote. 'In my opinion it is the lifts which are mainly responsible. I feel that all classes of players have become "lift conscious". The delaying tactics of the "A Class" players are communicated even to the "D Class". Here is an example to illustrate what I mean. A "D Class" player having over-rolled a hoop with his partner ball nearby shot away into a corner though the opponent's balls were at least ten yards apart from one another. I asked the reason for this and the player replied, "The good players always do that; I am watching them carefully to learn tactics." Little wonder that games take so long to finish. The lifts were, I believe, started to give the out-player a chance. They became absurd when, as so often happens, both players have been in half-a-dozen times. The new players of post-war croquet have no idea of what a good game of croquet was before the lifts were introduced.'

Despite this outburst against the system he had devised, DD was a frequent guest at the Rev. Elvey's home at Willingdon, near Eastbourne. His widow, Nora, herself a class player, remembers these times clearly but not without a shot of criticism for DD's style on the lawns. 'She was a dull player,' she recalls with some emphasis, 'a hitter, if you know what I mean.' In Nora's recollection, the great DD was also 'a little strait-laced'. It sounds like a polite understatement.

DD was also an excellent horsewoman – she hunted regularly during the winter – and an enthusiastic bell-ringer who, according to Nora, 'had even rung abroad'. But, for all her accomplishments, she does not seem to have been the jolliest of house guests and it is not surprising that the young Nora preferred livelier company such as that of the beautiful and graceful Mrs Ionides who won the Women's Championships in 1931.

DD held her mallet with a tight grip which, according to Maurice Reckitt, 'looked as if it must have involved a great deal of strain' and in the end, it was her wrists which gave way and forced her to concentrate less on playing and more on managing tournaments. This she seems to have done with the same degree of determination and zeal as she had brought to playing. The gazette records her bemoaning the problems of the modern-day manager. 'I have managed a number of tournaments, both before and since the war, and find that now it is impossible to get through a tournament in the time allowed unless the number of entries is at least two-thirds less than it was before the war,' she wrote.

No doubt she did her best to encourage the players to speed things up. Psychology seems to have been her really strong point. She was not a great hoop runner though her split shots were apparently accurate enough to help make up for it. Where she succeeded above all else was in going out for a game and winning against all odds. As such, she was a valuable addition to international Test teams and played for Great Britain in the first ever match against Australia in 1925, held at Roehampton. However, when she was invited to join the team for the return contest in Australia in 1926–7, she refused to go unless her expenses were paid. The matter was resolved but on this occasion, she was not at her best. Affected by the heat, she lost two of her games, which in turn, lost Great Britain the contest. In New Zealand where the team went for a short visit after Australia, she again lost but ten years later, she did better in the triangular Test match played in England.

She died in January 1965, aged eighty. She had lived with her unmarried sister Evelyn (also a croquet player) and her battles over expenses had contributed to an impression that the two ladies might be financially hard-up. Prichard's notes however, record that when Evelyn died nine years later, she left the not inconsiderable sum of £120,000.

Miss Steel had few equals in the game. Her nearest rival amongst the women during the Twenties appears to have been Noel Gilchrist. Reckitt describes how Miss Gilchrist first appeared on the Riviera, and without having had any practice, won the Opens at Menton. She went on to dominate the ladies' game during the next season winning at Ranelagh and Devonshire Park where not even DD could stop her. They teamed up for the Open Doubles Championships which they won twice in 1927 and 1928, Miss Gilchrist playing under her married name of de la Motte. She died in December 1967, having given up croquet long before, though still fondly remembered for her 'graceful style' and her 'natural' talent for the game.

After 1945, three ladies came to the fore of the women's game – Mrs E. Rotherham, Miss E. J. Warwick and Miss D. A. Lintern. Daisy Lintern emerged from the depths of Somerset to play in her first tournament in 1925 but it was not until 1949 that she first won the Women's Championship, going on to win it a further four times. She is remembered now, less for her croquet ability, considerable though this was, than for a mild eccentricity in her style of play which demonstrated itself in the odd habit of kicking up one leg when she struck the ball. She was a fierce defender of this game she loved so much and went out of her way to shield it from any invasion by 'unsuitable' newcomers. Memories of her appearance still cause some ripples of amusement in the then younger generation who knew her, for she was a dumpy creature who wore a hat and spectacles which made her look exactly like the granny in Giles' famous cartoons.

Former opponents remember her as a good 'solid' player but she was also a formidable administrator and in 1958, she achieved a singular triumph, to date, when she became the first ever (and only) female Chairman of the Croquet Council. This was, perhaps, her crowning year for she won the Mixed Doubles Championship for the fourth (and last) time in partnership with Maurice Reckitt. There are delightful stories of Daisy in her later years turning up for tournaments at unheard of hours of the morning because she had confused the time and of her driving her small green car across the cricket pitch at Hurlingham, having taken a wrong turning on the way out. But though she might, like all the best people, have grown mildly dotty with age, her love of croquet never diminished and she gave a great deal of encouragement and enthusiasm to other players.

By this time, the ladies were a diminishing band. Only two of them, Joan Warwick and Mrs Rotherham fought a duel for supremacy in the early Sixties. Both had played successfully in Test matches, Mrs Rotherham a total of three times. She had come into the game early in life during the Thirties, unlike Miss Warwick who took up croquet only after having first achieved considerable success as an international hockey player. Whereas Miss Warwick's play was of a cautious, unremarkable style, Mrs Rotherham's was described as 'majestic'. In 1960, she won the Opens, becoming only the third woman to do so, the other two being Mrs Beaton and DD Steel. Apart from an interesting backswing which apparently always went crooked, her great distinction was her immaculate costume. According to Elizabeth (Betty) Prichard, she would arrive on the lawn 'dressed as if she was going to a cocktail party. Earrings, make-up, net on her hair, very tidy and very beautifully turned out.'

Another lady of great elegance was Lydia Elphinstone Stone. Until she died in 1963, she spanned almost the entire historical period of English croquet. Born in 1866, she first played at Maidstone in 1895 and was holder of the Ladies' Challenge Cup in 1897 which she lost a year later in her struggle against Lily Gower. She was still active in 1961 but perhaps her most distinctive appearance was against the young John Solomon in 1948 when he made his debut at Hurlingham and played Miss Elphinstone Stone, then sixty-six years his senior. Elizabeth Prichard has an interesting memory of seeing the great Mrs Beaton (Lily Gower) watching a tournament, accompanied by a young man who might have been her son. Finding the courage to ask 'the boy' if his companion was indeed the great lady, Betty Prichard found herself talking to the young Solomon but she declined his offer of an introduction to one of croquet's greatest players, feeling perhaps slightly intimidated by the fact that she wore 'a huge hat with a great dome on top'.

By the Sixties, the women's game was definitely in decline. Three men, Cotter, Hicks and Solomon, dominated British croquet and one of them, E. P. C. Cotter, says without a trace of chauvinism, that they simply raised the game to a higher standard.

Contemporary player Veronica Carlisle (three times winner of the Women's Championship) who, having played against Daisy Lintern and Joan Warwick, bridges the past and the present, feels that ladies did better when croquet was played by the leisured classes, simply because they had fewer responsibilities in the home. Debbie Cornelius, the only leading lady in the current youthful generation of British players, feels differently. For her, the main reason for the lack of female players at the top is that the women are no longer prepared to make the effort to compete on equal terms. 'They allow themselves to be introduced to the game by husbands whose own play overshadows their own and at club level, they are happy enough to make organizing the tea come first and put playing croquet second.'

In her determination to win, Debbie has much in common with many of the earlier female champions, but in appearance she seems to resemble one in particular. 'Although of Lilliputian size, Kitty Sessions was a pocket Hercules who played an enterprising and powerful game with a mallet almost as tall as herself,' wrote Prichard. He might have been describing Debbie Cornelius.

The daughter of a croquet player, Debbie learnt her game on summer holidays at a hotel in Norfolk. There she played with her father and brother Stephen until she was eighteen. One summer, they all entered their first official tournament and the family came away with honours. Debbie went on to win the Women's Championship in 1988 and in 1989 achieved the distinction of being the first woman since Betty Prichard in 1975, to be selected for the Chairman's Salver. She is rightly acknowledged as 'the best woman player we have had for a number of years'.

In her brief summer shorts and peaked golfing cap, she looks a far cry from the gloved and hatted creatures of almost a hundred years ago who held a mallet in one hand and a parasol in the other. Yet she shares with those early women a daintiness mixed with unyielding determination to win in a game she also regards as an intellectual challenge. Lily Gower would probably have agreed with Debbie Cornelius when she summarizes her reasons for playing croquet by saying: 'I like the tactics. I like having to think. I like the fact that when you are on the lawn it's basically you against you and you can almost forget the other person because if you don't do it right, it doesn't matter what he does.'

The September edition of the 1989 croquet gazette, *Croquet*, addressed itself to the question of 'Who is the best woman player in the world?' The (unsigned) writer noted that during the Thirties, DD Steel had not only proved herself the best woman player but had also excelled over many of the men. From 1922 until 1964 (apart from the war years) at least one woman had competed annually in the President's Cup – a prestigious invitation event for the best eight or ten players available. However, since 1964, only one woman, a New Zealander has been selected. Debbie Cornelius will doubtless soon change all this. At present, she belongs to a small international field of women players which includes Madeline Hadwin of New Zealand and Carolyn Spooner and Creina Dawson of Australia. One of the few to have seen all four women play is New Zealand champion Bob Jackson who ranks Madeline Hadwin and Debbie Cornelius top. Men dominate the game in New Zealand but in Australia, the Ladies' Singles Championship still attracts a reasonable entry. Started in 1970, it has been won three times by Creina Dawson of South Australia and Mary Grieve of Victoria and twice by Carolyn Spooner (and also by Lorraine Bray of Queensland). The number of entries reached an all-time high in 1978 with a total of sixty. It has now settled to more or less half that number.

Meanwhile, Debbie occupies a lonely position in British croquet. A few others have come and gone, Jan McLeod being perhaps the most significant in the Eighties but few have had the 'pertinacity' to keep up the challenge. It seems strange that the game should have had so many fine women players and now have so few and the theory that the lack of domestic help is the cause seems hardly sufficient. After all, household chores and bringing up children do little to keep women from work. Croquet is a highly competitive sport and with the present domination by men, it takes a tough personality to challenge them on equal terms. Several young women have tried it in recent years but none have had the success of Miss Cornelius. The croquet character is an unusual and interesting phenomenon and it may be that contemporary women prefer to channel the sort of undiluted determination required to compete at the very top in more lucrative fields – such as politics. Alternatively, it may simply be that in general, the ladies are less complicated than the men.

THE CROQUET CHARACTER

The croquet 'character' is a curious one. The requirements include an ability to think logically, to be philosophical, patient, determined and resolute – and be prepared to discard all this on a whim in pursuit of a brilliant tactical idea. Caution competes with flair. The will to win must often bow to a bitter acceptance that fate occasionally seems to take a hand and turns a winning streak into incomprehensible disaster. Unlike tennis, where a bad shot is forgotten by the end of the following serve, in croquet a competitor is sometimes forced to sit and contemplate his errors while the opponent makes the most of them. At times, the game breeds introspection. The best players can be sensitive souls, often solitary and sometimes strange. As Arthur Lillie wrote, 'the nervous temperament which produces very brilliant play has its moments of depression as well as of exhilaration'.

The game's reputation for mild eccentricity feeds on itself and draws individuals (male and female alike) of an independent and, often rather obstinate disposition. However, unlike the dramas often played out in professional tennis, croquet players are not usually given to fits of pique in the middle of tournaments. Accounts of sudden outbursts of uncontrolled feeling, (a mallet driven hammer-like into a lawn or hurled into a hedge in utter frustration) do exist, but only because they are rare enough to excite special mention. In general, the most emotion likely to be witnessed during play is demonstrated in a slight tightening of the lips, a puzzled shake of the head, or, in extreme cases, a clenching of fists. Off the lawns however, a strange transformation takes place and this admirable restraint is tossed aside with astonishing abandon.

Throughout its history, the Council of the Croquet Association has witnessed a series of internecine wars in which members have gone out of their way to 'draw blood' over differences which were often petty and trivial. Those who are unable to reach the level of Council politics have contented themselves with seething correspondence which foams forth in the pages of the gazette (and has even occasionally overflowed into the national press), conducting furious battles plotted in pen and ink between members of all ages, from home and abroad. This spirit of contention is something of a time-honoured tradition which goes back to the very beginnings of English croquet.

Walter Jones Whitmore was undoubtedly a 'character' having large quantities of both individuality and obstinacy which often left him at odds with his fellow croquet players. His story has been related in some detail earlier (along with that of some of the ladies who might otherwise have been noted here) but one of his most careful biographers and perhaps the first to openly recognize both Walter's 'versatility' and his lack of stability, was the Reverend G. F. H. Elvey. The latter produced a full account of Walter Jones Whitmore for the gazette in 1960. This article, much quoted but not always acknowledged, was reprinted in a 1967 edition to mark the centenary of the Croquet Association. Sadly, on this occasion, it also marked the year in which the Rev. Elvey died.

Let it be said at once that the Reverend Elvey was one exception that proved the rule. Individual he undoubtedly was – not many people are blessed with the sort of resounding Christian names which commemorate a popular composer – but George Frederick Handel Elvey managed to contribute a great deal to both the administration and the playing of the game without upsetting his fellow players. True, his introduction of the lifting system caused distress to Miss Steel but few could really quarrel with a man who began his contributions to the gazette (as no doubt he did his Sunday sermons) with the uplifting words, 'Well, it is nice to be on the lawn again, and happily it is a pleasant day . . . Now about those roquets.'

The Reverend Elvey always appeared on the croquet lawns in clerical black, flapping across the grass like a corpulent crow. His was a long and happy association with the game for he joined the CA in 1902 and only left it when he died some sixty-five years later. (His widow Nora, a lively young woman in her nineties, currently lives in Oxfordshire, surrounded by photographs of a beaming and cherubic Handel.) His best playing years coincided with those of the Irish invasion of Corbally, O'Callaghan and Duff Mathews but some thirty-five years later, he won a tournament in Eastbourne at Devonshire Park and was still competing when in his seventies. Most of his clerical life was spent in Sussex and this seems to have provided many of his and Nora's happiest croquet moments for it is the period that his wife now remembers best. He was a skilled carpenter and made mallets for both of them and also wrote two books on croquet, one of which *Croquet: a handbook on the strokes and tactics of the game*, (1949) offered an interesting variation on the question of origins. He suggested that croquet was merely a form of 'lawn billiards' 'since on good authority Billiards was once an outdoor game, and the earliest tables retained croquet characteristics in the shape of a peg – called 'the king' – and a hoop on the centre line of the table'.

Elvey was Chairman of the Croquet Council between 1939 and 1948 and his contribution to copies of the gazette covered a variety of topics. On the matter of the laws and tactics, they were little short of inspirational. His optimism did much to help the Association recover itself after war – both the first and the second. Towards the end of his playing career he appears to have slowed down considerably. 'He walked appallingly badly with a stick,' says one who remembers him well. 'When he was playing doubles with Nora, he'd say, "You go and play this one Nora and leave me nearer" (the hoop). So off she would trot – she was terribly energetic – and he used to sit watching in his shiny, fustian black – black coat, black hat, black gaiters, black everything. No matter how hot the day, he was always dressed like that.' He seems to have suffered from the slightest change of temperature as when walking between the two croquet clubs, near to each other in the seaside town of Eastbourne he used to say, 'If I go up to Compton Nora, I think I'll take another coat. Compton's always a coat colder than down at Devonshire Park.'

His clerical ways did not please everyone. His departure from Cheltenham coincided with the decision to allow play there on Sundays (previously banned, along with dogs and children). On hearing of his decision, the then Secretary of Cheltenham was heard to murmur. 'That'll be a blot off the landscape.'

However, in general, his views were respected and he got on well with his fellow croquet players, steering Council through some of its stormier moments with great patience and fortitude. This was not so with several of his contemporaries.

Known for a rather irascible nature, Lord Tollemache seemed to take delight in disrupting affairs, especially those of the Croquet Council. Tollemache began his play in Cheshire, arriving at the Open Doubles in 1910 and announcing, somewhat ambitiously for a new-comer, that he would triple peel his opponent and peg him out – which he did. As the years progressed, he changed his stance from side to centre play and provided the world in general with details of his forth-right views on how the game should be conducted in the form of two books. The first of these was an elaborately illustrated volume published in 1914, full of photographs, demonstrating in minute detail Tolle-mache's opinions on conducting the game. The second was produced in Eastbourne after the Second World War where his lordship had defiantly remained throughout the enemy action. *Modern Croquet, Tips and Practice* appeared as a result of the author's conviction of the need for a revival of 'really professional' croquet. The preface urges upon the reader the importance of daily practice: 'Why not have a ball and mallet in your room? Short roquets can be played, aimed at a sixpence on the carpet. The ball can be stopped by a cushion. You can now practise the shot, which runs a four-foot hoop, every day at odd moments.'

One of his favourite strokes was the 'Jump Shot' which he averred was 'the prettiest shot in the game'. Quite clearly, croquet was his passion and he passed on his theories and opinions with equal depths of feeling, his writings spattered with enthusiastic exclamation marks and often accompanied by rousing cries of 'Good Hunting!' He died in 1955 at the age of seventy, remembered for devotion to the game and his 'strong, vigorous personality'.

Another such uninhibited member of the upper classes was Viscount Doneraile, an Irish peer, who like Tollemache, was perhaps more singular in his dedication to the game than in his play. Maurice Reckitt relates that Doneraile had a long career involving various sporting bodies and his thoughts only became 'concentrated on croquet' during his later life. He was particularly keen on involvement at Hurlingham where his interventions often bordered on the authoritarian. He had a habit of arbitrarily cancelling matches if they did not suit his personal timetable and was said to keep a private store of 'peach-fed ham and perry' at Hurlingham, which he doled out to his favourite acquaintances. In the late Thirties he wrote a foreword to A *Handbook on Modern Croquet* produced by the CA, full of wondering rhetorical questions and a few thrilling anecdotes told with an obvious gift for gentle elaboration and the sort of enthusiasm not out of place in a boy's adventure comic. 'We are often told that one half the world does not know how the other half lives: the allegation is sadly out of proportion in the case of the players of the game of Croquet,' he announced grandly. 'For who would suppose that some hundreds of people spend most of the summer travelling about the country and playing in tournaments.' Who indeed.

After a particularly good meal, Lord Doneraile is said to have fallen off the bridge into the lake at Hurlingham thereby prompting the reconstruction of the bridge with the side barriers which remain today. However, the history of the Hurlingham Club states the present bridge, complete with barriers, was constructed after its predecessor was swept away in the disastrous flood of 1928. Another good story recounted by Prichard, tells how the daughter of the first Viscount became the only female member of the freemasons. Caught eavesdropping from inside a clock, she was enrolled expressly in order to preserve their secrets.

Doneraile and Tollemache were comparatively minor thorns in the flesh of the Council. Others were much more troublesome. An early example was H. F. Crowther Smith, a talented writer and artist whose cartoons illustrated many early copies of the gazette and also his book *The Art of Croquet* published in 1932. In 1914, Crowther Smith reached his peak, gaining a place in the Best Ten players (an early form of ranking) and winning the Challenge Cup at Woking – which he promptly refused to return until such time as the end of the war and a return to normal playing practice, would allow him to defend it. After furious threats of litigation and piqued resignation from the CA, Crowther Smith finally gave up the cup four years later but his conduct had so incensed the Council that they refused to reinstate him until he apologized. According to Prichard, he finally did, capitulating some six years later. After that, he was gradually restored to the bosom of the CA, becoming editor of the gazette in 1937 which post he retained until 1954. He also wrote a book on *The Art of Golf Croquet* and continued to report on CA tournaments almost to his death in May 1959 at the considerable age of eighty-six.

In general, the aberrations of characters like these were tolerated with mild humour and once they were dead, confined to history. Their occasional deviations from the norm were rarely questioned in public as croquet, like the best 'families', likes to close ranks around its members however questionably they may have behaved. Few are exposed 'warts and all', and few have aroused such contradictory and impassioned emotion as Bryan Lloyd Pratt.

Lloyd Pratt's obituary in the 1983 edition of the gazette is quite extraordinary in its length and depth of feeling. It covers more than a full page; an exceptional degree of tribute (and barely suppressed censorship) for a man who was adored and despised with equal fervour and of whom both friends and enemies still talk in remarkably guarded terms.

Bryan Lloyd Pratt was born a conundrum. Adopted from an orphanage at an early age he was apparently brought up in complete luxury, a veritable Little Lord Fauntleroy who was even selected to make a charity presentation to the last royal patron of all debutantes, Queen Mary. However, his relations with his adopted parents were not, it seems, very happy. He did not get on with his adopted father and his adopted mother died, which left the unfortunate Bryan with an adopted stepmother whom he despised. Not, one would imagine, the most encouraging arrangement for an insecure young man already confused about his origins.

He went to Uppingham and from there to Emmanuel College, Cambridge. Roger Schlesinger, the former publisher and brother of the film director John Schlesinger, was at school and university with Lloyd Pratt and remembers him with interest: 'He was an extraordinary character. Witty, clever, a natty dresser, apparently homosexual, and a very good cellist.'

After university, Lloyd Pratt inclined towards the church but then veered away in favour of the stage. He joined a small repertory company but later abandoned it in preference for a job as a schoolmaster.

It was in 1955 that he reputedly first encountered croquet. He was watching a tennis tournament at Hunstanton when a nearby croquet match caught his attention. He joined the club immediately and in

1959, made his first appearance in the President's Cup (which was won by John Solomon). In 1963, he played in the Test match series against New Zealand and Australia. On fast lawns, his delicate touch came into its own and on this occasion, he was undefeated in the series of singles games he played. He was a stylish player launching himself, writes Prichard, 'on the ball of one foot and the toe of the other'. Maurice Reckitt also conceded that Lloyd Pratt was a 'class' player but added, 'It is not further skill but steadiness, even in the simplest physical sense, that he needs to cultivate.'

But steadiness does not often go with vivacity and Lloyd Pratt was either 'up' or 'down'. In top form, whether playing or socializing, he could be quite brilliant. The ladies in particular remember his elegance and gaiety with a certain wry affection. Lloyd Pratt accompanied them on their seasonal tour of the clubs commonly known as 'the circuit', invariably appearing on the lawns in his straw hat, coloured 'yellow', according to the waspish little limerick that once appeared about him, though also sometimes pink and grey. He also liked cravats and wore them in Noël Coward style. 'He was a character you know,' says Vera Tyrwhitt-Drake whose own husband, the six-foot-eight 'Tiny' was not unremarkable on the lawns. 'There's no doubt about it, if he went to a tournament, it did somehow seem to get a lift. He was so amusing and full of vitality.' However, he also had a reputation for being rather tart and could abruptly terminate his flow of charm with an icy remark which cut to the quick.

His sharp tongue upset everyone from time to time, as did his silly, simpering behaviour on and around the lawns. 'Do ask Bryan to go away, he's giggling at us,' the little old ladies would plead as he sniggered on the sidelines. But in general the women were tolerant of his little ways. Less so the men, especially when he decided to take part in croquet 'politics'.

In 1970, Lloyd Pratt was appointed editor of the gazette and when his first edition appeared it was to gasps of general amazement. Here was sport as art. The production had imposing Gothic titles, a more expensive weight of paper and a cover featuring the 'Rape of Roquetetta', (the first 't' silent), a pre-Raphaelite female languidly trailing a mallet, who had first appeared on the frontispiece of Leonard Williams' book *Croquet*, in 1899.

In Lloyd Pratt's opinion, this creature had 'come to stand for the more endearing . . . enduring qualities of our fascinating game'.

Moreover, she epitomized his personal romantic fantasy of croquet which took scant regard of such mundane practicalities as finance.

In this, Lloyd Pratt was respecting the time-honoured tradition inaugurated by Walter Jones Whitmore who had also demonstrated a total lack of interest in 'sums'. Worse, however, Lloyd Pratt's provocative editorial content strongly offended his 'management'.

He had a thundering Colonel Blimp style which compelled attention. Few could ignore headlines which demanded 'Survival, Expansion or Decline' or 'England seems, temporarily let it be hoped, to have gone mad.' And few could ignore the bees in his bonnet which he used to sting his audience into reaction.

One was the question of playing sport in South Africa. Using the political ban on cricket test matches as his starting point, Lloyd Pratt sent a message to his 'fellow croquet-playing South Africans' that they would always be welcomed in England. It received a warm response from South Africa but a cooler response at home. Undeterred, Lloyd Pratt went on to breathe fire into another dragon, that of popularizing croquet. He was fiercely against the idea, claiming, with some justification that 'if croquet is to survive, it must be true to itself'. But on this subject, comments crept into his editorials which smacked of the sort of 'class jealousy' which others deplored. Words like 'privilege', 'luxury', 'an atmosphere of disdain and exclusiveness', the suggestion that the game be confined to 'the sort of people, to put the matter bluntly, whom it will be a pleasure to meet at tournaments' echoed uncomfortably through the pages of the gazette.

In fairness, such snobbery is not unheard of in the croquet world but Lloyd Pratt's mistake was to use the gazette to express his personal opinions so boldly. In an article entitled 'Croquet and the British Tax payer' he fiercely denounced 'government-sponsored coaching schemes' and the tone, once light and witty, became spiteful and lecturing, upsetting many of his readers. Oscar Wilde was invoked in defence of the argument but Lloyd Pratt's conclusion that croquet, being an esoteric sport for intellectuals could never be popularized without vulgarizing it, was a puffed up piece of nonsense.

It was a pity. His views may well have been shared by a few but the immoderation with which Lloyd Pratt expressed them infuriated many. They also sadly obscured a literary style that was worthy of a wider audience and which made a welcome change between the pages of the gazette where, all too often down the years, lists of competitions and somewhat dry reporting of events have tended to exclude the finer turn of phrase.

With the deliberate intention of keeping 'tournament results down to a tolerable proportion', Lloyd Pratt introduced a retrospective collection of articles called 'As it Was'. This series sparkled with the glitter of name-drops. It provided more gossip than croquet information about his subjects, (one of his interviews, with Lady Julian Parr, blissfully omitted most of the sporting details about her, including the fact that she had startled the croquet world by soaring to fame in the Northern championships in 1900 at the tender age of thirteen) but did give some interesting insights into the Edwardian game. Likewise, the poems that were published under Lloyd Pratt's editorship, constructed on models varying from Hilaire Belloc to Robert Graves, also added to the 'literary' style of his editions.

However, like all flamboyant and brilliant editors, Lloyd Pratt attracted too much attention and quickly made enemies. Increasingly, his opponents rallied to the assault, choosing as their primary line of attack the subject of finance. It became increasingly clear that Lloyd Pratt was a luxury they felt they could not afford. A Council meeting in 1970 had questioned the finances with, as Lloyd Pratt reported in his next gazette, 'ugly words like "cheaper paper", "offset lithography" and "cutting our coat according to our cloth"'. All too soon, the rumblings grew into outright protest but Lloyd Pratt foolishly continued to ignore them and to tactlessly alienate the opposition. Finally, however, the question of the rising running costs of the magazine defeated him. After editing only four editions, his resignation was called for and though he fought it out in the pages of *The Times* and the *Sunday Times*, claiming that his dismissal was due to editorial critical of Council policy, by doing so, he only succeeded in placing himself more firmly beyond the pale.

In 1970, he had visited South Africa as a coach and he now decided to emigrate there. He was warmly welcomed into the Rondebosch Club where he served on the committee and acted as a tournament manager. He is also said to have spent some time teaching ballroom dancing in Cape Town. He died in South Africa in 1983, surrounded by scandalous stories fuelled by speculation about his rapid departure from England and his financial situation after his house mysteriously caught fire and about other aspects of his personal life. 'It was all hearsay,' his champions say today. The recorded facts are that he was stabbed to death at the age of fifty-two by 'a young acquaintance after a fierce struggle'.

It was a curious end for one of croquet's more colourful characters. As a player, he was undoubtedly talented. He played side-style, using a long mallet with a long head and his stop shots were legendary. So was his doubles play. Players who partnered him were delighted by his insistence on 'democratic doubles' in which he refused to dominate a game.

He is still remembered with a mixture of fondness and fury. Some cannot forget or forgive his acid tongue. Others can only recall his undeniable charm. 'How sad to know that Bryan is no longer with us,' wrote one. 'He was a character and there are all too few characters in croquet today.'

Humphrey Hicks only outlived Lloyd Pratt by a few years but he was certainly another of croquet's 'colourful characters'.

H. O. Hicks was born in 1904 in Esher, Surrey. His mother and father both played croquet, as did his two brothers. Humphrey was educated at Dartmouth for a naval career which, eventually, he did not pursue. In 1930 he won the Champion Cup (now the President's Cup) and in 1932, the Open Championships. It was not until after the Second World War that he hit top form, returning to the game to win the Open Championships from 1947 to 1952, the President's Cup five times, the Men's Championships nine times, the Men's Doubles eight times and the Mixed Doubles four times. He played in three Test series and was known for his sharp tactics. His own special eccentricity was his habit of doing a bit of 'handiwork' during matches, while waiting for his turn. Prichard refers to this as 'needlework' but both Veronica Carlisle, former Women's Champion and Vera Tyrwhitt-Drake, a frequent spectator at tournaments where Humphrey played, state quite firmly that it was knitting. So do Nora Elvey and Patrick Cotter. The latter played against Humphrey on more than one occasion and adds that his strategy of appearing to be more involved in his knitting than in the play of his opponent 'did not fool me one bit!'

Described by some as 'rather an aloof character', Hicks, like Lloyd Pratt, had more to him than met the casual eye. Unmarried, he apparently took an interest in helping poor families. 'He would be playing and suddenly a rush of children would arrive at the Club,' recalls one player. It seems these would be waifs and strays belonging to some family which Humphrey had taken up and they would vanish again almost as suddenly as they appeared. Humphrey himself was a constant presence on the croquet lawn and was at various times a member of Hurlingham, Budleigh Salterton Lawn Tennis and Croquet Club and Sidmouth Cricket and Tennis Club. Wherever he was, his behaviour was invariably the same. 'You would see him walk in, a hat on his head and no doubt a knitting bag in his hand and he would find a solitary place to park his chair then he would sit there and knit.'

Prichard complained that in later life, Humphrey became 'something of a prima donna'. His intolerance of bad manners about the court was legendary and was sometimes taken to extremes. Edgar Jackson, a long-term member of Cheltenham, remembers an occasion when Humphrey halted play 'steaming with rage' because his opponent had been temporarily called away to the telephone. But he was one of the greatest players of his time as well as one of the greatest characters in croquet and if, as his obituary in the gazette says, he was often 'outspoken in his condemnation of the slightest breach of etiquette; he was at the same time a valued friend'. He continued to take an interest in croquet right up to his death in June, 1986.

Edgar Jackson is the last of these great 'dinosaurs'. He and his wife now live in a house constructed in the garden of their former home. One room of the otherwise 'ordinary' house dominates, filled by a magnificent full-size snooker table and the Cheltenham Croquet Club lies a gentle stroll away from a back door in their garden. They are a delightful couple. Edgar is full of mild criticism about the contemporary game, his wife Joan is an intelligent, gentle prompter on recollections of past triumphs in Edgar's long croquet career. A first-class player (he won the Men's Championships twice), his greatest contribution to the game has been in changing the croquet calendar to make room for weekend tournaments so that the'working man' might have an equal chance to participate alongside the retired and the independently wealthy. In connection with this move to greater democracy on the lawns, he also introduced the 'Swiss' formation to croquet where players all have the same number of games, thereby offering an alternative to the knockout system in which a player might take holiday for a whole week only to find himself disqualified from a tournament after his first game. Edgar also introduced the Bray system, named after Dr Roger Bray, then Chairman of the Laws Committee, to shorten the length of time of games. 'All my interest has been in making tournaments enjoyable for people who aren't very good and to arrange equal play,' he says. His other great contribution to croquet has been his work as a tournament manager.

From Devonshire Park to Budleigh Salterton, Edgar has managed tournaments with unfailing efficiency, but nowhere so gladly perhaps as in his own beloved Cheltenham. He is a familiar sight each year when the Men's Championships are held there. A great reader of Victorian novels, he has a Victorian air himself with his long white side whiskers and his craggy head. Never saying a great deal, he misses very little. He has two present anxieties about the game. One is that too many championships are crowding croquet. 'Today, the only people who matter are the people who win and I think that croquet is about people who play,' he says, echoing a complaint that has clouded British croquet since it became an 'official' game. The second is that contemporary croquet players should remain 'pleasant, gracious chaps who behave properly'. Writing in the gazette in 1983, he summed up the paradox of the croquet 'character' with the words, 'Isn't it a bore? We all think we are unique. It has even been said that you have to be an individualist to play the game at all. What a shame!'

Maurice Reckitt noted in defence of the croquet character that 'croquet, by its very nature, will only be played by those who love it'. For years, Reckitt dominated the croquet scene. His brother, Geoffrey, was reportedly a far better croquet player and few, it seems could have had a worse style than Maurice. His action on the lawns was described as 'notoriously inconsistent and somewhat temperamental'. Nonetheless, he produced a book for beginners called *Croquet Today* which contains several good instructional passages and a lot of distilled croquet wisdom.

Reckitt played his first tournament at St Leonards on Sea in 1908. Thereafter, he was a regular visitor to the south coast until the early Seventies, when age and illness finally slowed him down. He died in January 1980, at the age of ninety-one, his longevity a defiance of medical wisdom which had labelled him 'a sickly youth'. Ill-health had prevented him serving in the First World War and from joining up with the family firm that later merged with Colman's of Norwich. He went to Wellington College and from there up to Oxford where he read Modern history at St John's. Sometime later, in the Seventies, a club was formed for Oxford graduates and Reckitt was more than pleased when asked if it might bear his name.

Quite how he started playing croquet, nobody seems to know. After that first appearance in 1908, he became such a regular part of the scene and such a force in Council life, that he seemed to have always been there. He was Chairman of the Council from 1937 to 1939 and Vice President from 1962 until 1967 in which year he succeeded the author and broadcaster, Sir Compton Mackenzie as President.

The same year, he welcomed the Queen to Hurlingham. It must have been a very proud occasion. Many are the photographs of Reckitt perched beside Her Majesty, instructing her on the play and no doubt whispering one of his famous asides which could be heard several feet away. In appearance, he represented the traditional image of a croquet player, tall, with military bearing, white hair and white moustache, yet croquet, however large it loomed, was only a part of his life.

He also appears to have enjoyed ballroom dancing and 'walking through the countryside' but his other great interest was Christian Sociology. He wrote or contributed to some fifty volumes on the subject, edited the quarterly *Christendom* and lectured throughout the country. His personal convictions seem to have made him something of a philosopher and this can be seen in some of his writing. Whether the problem was a transient one (over-crowding at tournaments or the difficulties of finding an experienced manager) or of more lasting significance, concerning the very future of the game, Reckitt treated his subject with respect. He was an historian and he brought an historian's perspective to much of what he wrote for the gazette. He was a regular contributor to the opinion column called 'Rover Notes', which he invented, but from time to time, reflection gave way to poetic licence. Reckitt produced some real doggerel, published under the pseudonyms of M. Bear and Ember. One of his most famous (largely because he seems to have quoted it at every possible occasion) was entitled 'The Big Four'. It celebrated the success of Patrick Cotter, John Solomon, Humphrey Hicks and Geoffrey Reckitt and wondered which of them would win the President's Cup in the following highly personal fashion:

'The champs come and go; it is tough at the top,
And the top's not a place where it's easy to stop.
Each age has its masters, both masculine and feminine
And "there were brave men before Agamemnon".'

Towards the end of his life, when he wasn't struggling for a rhyming line, Reckitt turned his pen to a history of croquet. It should have been a great work and it certainly runs to a large number of pages. Unfortunately, it rapidly became an extended 'minutes' of past tournaments and much of the text is a disappointingly dry account of match results. The typescript is kept by the Croquet Association (and is annotated in Reckitt's own spidery hand). Despite its limitations, it has certainly provided a background for more than one author in search of 'a bit of history' – which in fact, is what Reckitt had hoped. He wrote to the gazette telling the editor that his *History of Croquet*, was in fact 'a series of annals' stretching from the mid-Nineties of the last century to the mid-Sixties of this one. His greatest hope was that someone else might take up the work and turn it into a more readable form and, in the introduction to his *The History of Croquet*, Prichard acknowledges Reckitt as 'the spur' which urged him to write his own book.

Reckitt divided his history into four phases. The first was croquet's emergence as a serious game under the guidance of Walter Jones Whitmore and friends. The second was croquet's great revival from 1894 to 1914 and here he makes an interesting historical point. In naming this as the heyday of croquet, Reckitt writes that 'croquet, often characterized as Victorian, could in fact be more truly seen as Edwardian'. He supports his argument with the fact that the King played croquet and that this was the era of the large country house party, of a flourishing leisured class and the arrival of the motor car which made travel about the countryside much more practical and which contributed to the increased popularity of the game. There is considerable evidence to show that he was right. Much of the revival in the Twenties and Thirties (Reckitt's third phase) coincided with a revival of society. Life between the wars was again fun and free as it had been in the Edwardian era. Reckitt's fourth phase, naturally began where he had left off after the Forties and ended in the Sixties – just too soon for him to appreciate the real turn of the wheel, when top players were once again thick on the ground and croquet had recovered a little of its social glamour.

Reckitt would have appreciated the 'fifth' cycle which has introduced so many new and young players to the game, not least, one imagines, because the present phase would have required him to do far less obituary writing. Penning a few lines on those who had passed on was one of Reckitt's most frequent contributions to the gazette. He was always fair, never speaking ill but often speaking honestly and with a hint of asperity which would catch the character exactly. Of Crowther Smith for example, he wrote with perfect balance 'apt to be headstrong and querulous at times, but a delightful companion and a notable wit'. A generous end-of-term report for one whose behaviour had sometimes caused the Council so much grief.

Reckitt's own recollection of 'croquet characters' was, almost inevitably, that there had been far more of the breed about in the past. He wrote an article on the subject, called 'Croquet as Comedy' and listed 'Donnie' (Lord Doneraile) as one of the most colourful personalities of the pre-war period. However, his account of one character who used to appear on the courts when he (Reckitt) was still a boy, is surely the best. Identified simply as 'Miss H', this formidable lady was driven round the countryside in a chauffeured car in which she was rumoured to have also slept. Arriving at the lawns dressed in a selection of odd garments, she would appear 'sometimes smoking a pipe and generally leading a black cat on a chain'. Her playing style seems to have been quite spectacular for Reckitt recalls a game against her in which he bent to put the clips on the hoop and looked up 'just in time to see her whirl her mallet round her head and take a slashing drive at the hoop'. He concluded that had he not had the agility to jump hastily aside, she would certainly have laid him out cold.

One doesn't see too much of this type of behaviour about the lawns today. Black cats are also rare. But croquet will always have its element of the unusual and try though it might to lose its image of the mildly absurd, it does so at the risk of also losing a part of its charm. As Reckitt wrote, 'Many men are sincerely devoted to their mothers-in-law, find nothing absurd in ordering a kipper for breakfast, and can pass through the sober town of Wigan without splitting their sides with laughter.' Their 'reputation' has simply become part and parcel of their character. Demolish the one and the unique quality of the other ceases to exist. The same is true of croquet.

Many other croquet players could be included here. Not least, those club members who were not very good at the game and therefore never appeared in the pages of the gazette but who 'knew everybody' and single-handedly kept their clubs going. Mrs Prichard remembers one lady in particular, Miss M. M. Paulley who for many years was a member of Cheltenham and acted as tournament secretary, organizing her first event in September 1927. She was a referee and handicapper and Chairman of the Club from 1957 to 1959 after which she requested not to be re-elected. She died in the late Sixties but 'she was the biggest character you've ever met,' says Elizabeth Prichard, organizing tournaments with a soft fist in an iron glove, barking at all and sundry, terrorizing newcomers and giving up both time and money to support the game she loved. 'When she finally gave up, they discovered she had paid for all the new balls from Jaques out of her own pocket.'

Contemporary croquet's most colourful characters continue the tradition of combining the essential ingredients of an element of intolerant brilliance soothed by wit and occasional charm. John Walters, Richard Hilditch and Keith Wylie all have at least one other element in common: they frequently express themselves in print. Keith Wylie can possibly lay greatest claim to this. His book *Expert Croquet Tactics* is a work which leaves all but the most determined behind. Reviewing it in the gazette, John Solomon confessed that on seeing the draft of the first few chapters he had expressed doubts that there would be an audience wide enough to justify its publication, as, for the most part it was 'pretty heavy-going despite the occasional flashes of wit'. Wylie's erudition, his brilliant play and his flashes of wit distinguish his contribution to croquet and it is sometimes hard to see where one element takes over from another. A letter to the gazette on the subject of his book, written a year after its review, said that sales of the first edition of 250 copies were 'well advanced' but that a few remained. Those who had 'held back' in the hope of securing a cut-price bargain were to be disappointed for he was about to raise the price to £21 plus £2 for postage and packing. Six oddly assembled editions remained of undoubted interest 'to amateur bookbinders' at the knock down price of £10 each 'or fifty pounds the lot'. History does not record if the great 'blockbuster' reading public were tempted.

A lean, tall man with a huge, domed forehead, Wylie has a delightfully dry sense of humour. In May 1984, he wrote a short article, complete with diagrams on the making of a croquet ball. A month later, he owned up to his practical joke. Not everyone, it seems, had realized that it was a spoof. In 1987, he wrote a long, detailed letter to the gazette about the problems of travelling by air with croquet mallets. To overcome the difficulty, he had had two trunks made to order. One 'is a really sturdy trunk that will last forever' but being somewhat too heavy for a single player, he had decided to donate it to the Croquet Association for use by any group of associate players going abroad. (It has since been used to transport mallets to test matches.) He went on to recommend the manufacturers of the second trunk, despite its rather cheap 'finish', who came from a trading estate in north London. Finally however, he revealed that he had discovered the perfect solution for carrying mallets – in a gun case. Filled with foam, 'it comfortably takes one full-length mallet plus one day's clothing and footwear'. Once again, Walter Jones Whitmore would have approved. Also a man of an 'inventive mind', his numerous contrivances had included a box designed so that mallets and balls could be securely held during travel.

Richard Hilditch and John Walters are the youngest of this croquet catalogue of the mildly 'unusual'. Richard Hilditch is a Cambridge graduate who knocked David Openshaw out of the draw for the Northern Championship in 1983 and went on to play a memorable game against Wylie, only to be finally defeated. With the years, he has grown, quite literally, in stature, so that details of his current appearances at tournaments may appear in the gazette under the heading 'Huge Quivering Bulk'. Generally distinguished by a floppy cotton hat (similar to that worn by Humphrey Hicks) and a grossly extended stomach, he has also been known to wear a pair of antenna about his ears. During the 1989 doubles tournament against New Zealanders Hogan and Jackson, Hilditch reportedly asked his opponents if they objected to this form of personal decoration. With typical antipodean forthrightness, Bob Jackson is said to have replied, 'I don't care if you play in your underpants'.

John Walters would never dream of such sartorial inelegance. Winner of the Chairman's Salver in 1985 (Lloyd Pratt won it in 1967), John used to wear bow ties to match the colour of his croquet balls. As editor of Townsend's *Croquet Almanack*, he has become a walking encyclopaedia of croquet records and folklore. Precise but passionate in his articles and correspondence in the gazette, he is elusive and something of a loner about the lawns. In 1980, the gazette records his appearance as a teenager at Hunstanton, in the company of the equally young Mark Avery and the very young (he was twelve) James Carlisle. 'One could not fail to be impressed by their impeccable lawn manners,' wrote the commentator. 'A tribute to their mentors and their parents.'

Yet the very eccentricity which sometimes marks out the croquet player can make them irritating beyond measure to those who have to deal with them in any other business than that of playing a game. With so many individualists stalking the lawns, small wonder that the administrative history of croquet is so riddled with strife.

Being 'colourful' implies a degree of independence of nature which will not always be endearing and this says much of croquet. No other game allows a man (or woman) to 'be himself' with such abandon. And no other game contains so many 'ordinary' players who are prepared to be so patiently tolerant of the determinedly different few.

The world of garden croquet boasts several characters who have made their name in other walks of life. Penelope Keith, Sir Michael Tippett, Magnus Pike, Patrick Moore, Brian Johnstone, Roy Hattersley, Sir Donald Sinden and newscaster Julia Somerville are all contemporary croquet players to name but a few. Like many others, Julia Somerville learnt to play on a lawn at home. 'It's a game for spoilers,' she says, adding, 'amazing how such a genteel game can rouse such terrible passions. The mallet is quite a brutal instrument and it often requires great restraint not to bash your opponent with it.'

One editor of the gazette wrote 'the only thing that all croquet players have in common is a love of croquet'. For most this is more than enough and serves to unite them countrywide.

THE CLUBS
The heartland of Association Croquet

E arly copies of the gazette are filled with announcements of fixtures for the year ahead, taking players through the length and breadth of the country and sometimes beyond. In one such calendar, published in 1906, games are listed in Scotland, (Edinburgh), Ireland (Black Rock, Co. Dublin and in Cork), Wales (Monmouthshire) and from Durham down to Bognor and Cheltenham to Reigate.

Life for many in those days seems to have been one happy, indolent game of croquet. Several clubs were founded in the 1860s but only came into force at the end of the century. One of the earliest clubs had been founded at Worthing by a Mr Harry Hargood who became the Hon. Secretary. Arthur Lillie set the date at 1865 but *The Field*, in an article in 1871, referred to a recent tournament at Worthing as 'one of the most successful meetings that has been held since the formation of the club in 1863'.

The annual subscription was a half guinea for one member, twenty-five shillings for a family of three and seven and sixpence for honorary members. On tournament days, refreshments and prizes were displayed in attractive tents and on one occasion, an Italian string band was lured from performance on Worthing pier, and induced to provide background music throughout the afternoon.

The said Harry Hargood is also credited with having started another croquet club in the grounds of the Brighton Pavilion. Here, according to Arthur Lillie, 'a famous ball was held every year, with the band of the Grenadier Guards as an attraction'. In Sussex, the then editor of *The Field*, John Hale, held court, (he was an equally fine tennis player and cricketer) and croquet clubs proliferated. The closest county rival (in number) was Gloucestershire, the original 'home' of the English game, where Lillie himself played a part in establishing a club.

'Mr Law was transferred from his curacy at Chipping Campden to be curate at one of the Cheltenham churches. From him I first learnt the game, and I was induced in the year 1869 to send out circulars for a croquet club. We had considerable difficulty about getting a ground. The Montpellier Gardens Committee were of the opinion that they could not give us any reserved portion and keep faith with their annual subscribers. But we induced them at last to give us a disused bowling green, which slightly enlarged, gave us two grounds, each thirty by twenty and of excellent turf.'

Wimbledon first opened its doors in Worple Road shortly after negotiations were completed in late 1869 for four acres of land to be leased for three years from a local solicitor. An illustration in *The Penny Illustrated Paper* of April 1871, shows several raised lawns, like giant catwalks, on which ladies and gentlemen stood about in crinolines, suits and tall hats and many more were seated around the sides under a variety of awnings. The extraordinary little thatched shelters, like African straw huts which were constructed to protect players from both sunshine and rain, appear to have been added later. By 1873, the Annual General Meeting of the All England Croquet Club could report that the yearly income at Worple Road was 'roughly estimated at a total of £200 a year, with a reasonable prospect of gradual augmentation'.

More new clubs soon sprang into being. By 1874, *The Field* was reporting meetings at Wirral Archery and Croquet Club, Torbay Archery and Croquet Club and Bedfordshire Croquet Club and South Bedfordshire? Many of the clubs were deliberately sited near to railway lines. These included Southwick and Parkstone which both lay in the lee of railway embankments, though travel to other clubs was often by horse and occasionally, as in the case of Shrewsbury, by ferry. The people of Budleigh Salterton in Devon formed a private company to bring the railway line closer to, among other things, the croquet club. Budleigh Salterton was also used as an archery and tennis club and held its first Open Croquet Tournament in 1896. Other new clubs included Compton in Eastbourne, Sussex which began life in 1898, Hunstanton in Norfolk which held its first tournament in 1913 and was the only club to continue playing throughout the First World War and, of course, Hurlingham.

Hurlingham House was built by Doctor William Cadogan in 1760. He had acquired nine acres of land from one of the Bishops of London who then had their summer residence at Fulham. Some years later, a Mr John Ellis purchased the property and began transforming Cadogan's original house into a neo-classic mansion. Completed in 1803, it forms the main part of the present Hurlingham clubhouse. In 1869, the house and part of the enlarged estate were leased to a Mr Frank Heathcote who formed the Hurlingham Club to accommodate his personal interest in pigeon-shooting (the club still retains a pigeon on its crest). Edward VII as Prince of Wales was a keen shot (and later on, a croquet player) and royal patronage ensured the club a future. In the same year that the Hurlingham Club opened its doors, the game of polo was introduced to England. In 1874, play began at Hurlingham which remained the headquarters of British polo until 1939, during which time the estate was once again extended, tennis and golf were introduced, and so was croquet.

The first croquet tournament was held in 1901. By the following year ten lawns had been made available and were considered the finest in England. In January 1928, the Thames burst its banks and flooded the grounds to a depth of six feet. The mud with which the courts were endowed at this time provided the foundation for an excellent quality of grass. Despite the occasional damage by marauding peacocks and, far more serious, the retirement of the head groundsman who had cared for the lawn for some fifty years until the early Seventies, standards at Hurlingham remain high. It is certainly England's most elegant setting for the game.

Perhaps croquet's finest moment was the visit of the Queen to Hurlingham in 1967. Her Majesty, who is Patron of the Croquet Association, came to present the All-England Centenary prizes. Three croquet lawns in front of Hurlingham House had been lovingly manicured by the head groundsman, Tom Grey, and were surrounded with chairs for spectators. A green trellis fence cordoned off a special enclosure containing four of the Hurlingham blue and white tents, in the centre of which stood the royal tent, fringed with gold and flanked by banks of blue hydrangeas. As the Queen appeared (dressed most appropriately in blue with white), the band of the Boys Brigade struck up the national anthem and the Royal Standard unfurled from the head of the flag pole. Her Majesty watched three of England's finest players in competition: John Solomon, Humphrey Hicks and Patrick Cotter.

Hurlingham has always been the grandest of the clubs. The tendency to do everything slightly better than anywhere else even extended to the catering. Nora Elvey remembers it with longing. 'They used to have lovely iced coffee with wads of cream on the top. It was delicious,' she recalls with a sigh.

Nora played regularly at Devonshire Park in East Sussex, another of the grand establishments of croquet which has now, sadly, closed its doors to the game. Nearby Compton took over from the Devonshire Park club when it closed to croquet some thirty years ago. Many still recall playing there in the post-war days when groups of the rich or retired went on 'the circuit', playing at tournaments up and down the country, croquet by day, bridge by night. Devonshire Park had been the darling of the croquet set in the early 1900s (there were 508 tournament entries in 1902) and for many, it retained its position as the last 'social' gathering of the croquet year, up until the very end. (It is now the site of the Pilkington Glass tennis championships.) A writer in the December 1971 gazette described the natural eagerness of players to 'seal or retrieve' their fortunes in the last fortnight of the season at Devonshire Park but added that for him, it was the people, not the play which made the place so special. There were the 'happy knots' of those behind the glass windows of the verandah, the 'silent watchers' on the balcony, the spectators stretched along the lee-side of the lawns and above all, the old friends 'immutably drawn back each year' and the new ones who would surely return. Devonshire Park was more than a home for the last tournament of the season; it was a social highlight of the happy croquet round.

Vera Tyrwhitt-Drake warmly recalls these halcyon days. Her husband, the six-foot-eight 'Tiny', came from croquet playing parents. He met his wife at Roehampton Club and after they married, they lived at Wimbledon, then Tunbridge Wells and finally settled in Eastbourne.

'We used to go to Cheltenham every year to play croquet. We stayed with Colonel and Betty Prichard in Wales and would drive every day from Gwent to Gloucestershire in two cars. David Prichard was absolutely besotted with the rules of croquet. They had a croquet lawn in the garden and they used to give a large house party.' Among the other guests would be the MP for Tonbridge Gerald Williams who died in January 1990 at the age of eighty-six. He was a familiar figure on the croquet lawns at Roehampton with his wife Lady Ursula.

These parties must have been a jolly time. Betty Prichard, the natural hostess, bright-eyed and vivacious with an infectious laugh and a wicked aptitude for mimicry, presided with the more serious Colonel over the gatherings at Gobion Manor. Most likely, they dined in the fine beamed room at the front of the house where a huge stone fireplace dominates one wall. They doubtless played croquet on the upper lawn in the garden, looking down over the green fields of Gwent, perhaps unaware that this was where Lt.-Colonel Harry Llewellyn (Mrs Prichard's cousin) schooled the legendary showjumper Foxhunter.

From here, they also went to Budleigh Salterton in Devon and to Hunstanton and the bracing air of Norfolk. Some, like Mrs Rotherham, did the entire south coast. Others were less adventurous and concentrated on a few great events but for all, Devonshire Park in Sussex 'was the last tournament at the end of the year'. Here, they enjoyed two weeks of constant croquet, interspersed only with evenings of bridge. Many stayed at the Grand Hotel in Eastbourne and all had a good time. 'It was marvellous!' says Betty Prichard. 'Terrible lawns. Everybody would grumble about them, but a wonderful two weeks.'

Before the war, life had been even more relaxing. The advent of the motor car had enabled players to transport themselves about the countryside at will. Few members of those who also constituted the 'croquet class' needed to work and when it was impossible to play croquet at home, the real devotees simply removed themselves to the South of France.

The early numbers of the gazette are full of advertisements for Menton and Hyères which seem to have been particularly popular centres. 'As soon as January came you went abroad,' recalls Vera. 'And what you did at home, you continued to do wherever else you went. You played croquet and bridge with exactly the same people! One of the perks was the fact that France was so cheap. You could live in a very nice hotel for absolutely nothing. In fact, everything was cheap. At home you could get a housemaid and a parlour maid and pay them a pittance. At Devonshire Park, everyone used to arrive with chauffeurs and servants to lay out their own picnics.'

But the clubs could turn to more serious matters when required. Ranelagh, now closed, was Vera's personal favourite as an attractive, friendly place in the Fifties. Much earlier during the First World War it was quick to volunteer its lawns for a game in aid of the Red Cross. Bowdon had a wartime sewing tournament and Roehampton, once the home of croquet until overshadowed by the more glamorous Hurlingham, called together a Voluntary Aid Committee which asked members to donate 'slipper pans, urinals, bed pans, bronchitis kettles, wheelchairs, stretcher-beds and crutches'.

After the Second World War many of the clubs which had temporarily closed, sadly remained so (see p.17) Others showed great fighting spirit and a determination to carry on whatever the difficulties. In 1941, Compton had four courts in action though no tournaments were arranged as the town of Eastbourne was closed to tourists. This ban on visitors in the coastal regions also affected Sussex County Club but in 1944, they were still playing seven courts and hoping 'military conditions permitting, to carry through all the usual Club competitions'. A year later in 1945, Compton reported that 'five years of wartime conditions have reduced the club to a state of suspended animation. During this period, four-fifths of the members have drifted away to safer areas; last year only ten remained and several of these rarely put in an appearance.' Half of the club's six lawns had had to be abandoned but the ban on coastal visitors had finally been lifted. Though it was unlikely that competitions could be resumed immediately, Compton eagerly informed members that 'visitors are assured at least of a warm welcome'. Compton had been helped over its difficulties by the Saffrons Cricket Club (to which it now belongs).

The Second World War was make or break for many of the clubs. Those which survived mostly grew in strength, and gradually, others have come to join the list. The 1989 Directory produced by the Croquet Association numbered 137 'registered' clubs and the numbers have grown again since then. Of these clubs, the 'giants' are those which still play host to Test matches and tournaments but whose reputation is not always confined to the quality of competition.

Food and drink have always had an important role in croquet club life, though contrary to popular belief, the menu rarely includes cucumber sandwiches or gin and tonic. The young players of today have more prosaic tastes in food, though Hurlingham still does a great trade in Pimms. In general, Colchester is famous for its lunches, Budleigh Salterton for its teas (and treacle tart) and Cheltenham for its bar. Many a croquet commentator, both past and present, official and unofficial, has made more than passing reference to the subject of refreshments. Maurice Reckitt was moved to poetry on the subject (once again!) and penned a West Sussex Tea Drinking song: (supposedly after the style of Hilaire Belloc but seeming to owe rather more to Noël Coward who was also a croquet player)

> Tea and Bun at Roehampton
> You'll get – but it's not too cheap;
> For scone and jam at Hurlingham
> The price is still more steep.
> At Budleigh now as I can avow,
> They've a splendid spread to show
> But the teas that are found on the Southwick ground
> Are the very best teas I know.

After food and drink, atmospheres have a great importance. A tournament reporter once remarked in the gazette that there was 'something about the air in Hunstanton which generates goodwill'. Certainly, many of the clubs are happy places and most can also claim fine settings. Budleigh Salterton, for example, once again caused Maurice Reckitt to burst into poetic rapture in the Seventies with a 'Sonnet for Salterton':

> Beloved spot! Known for many a year.
> Unrivalled for variety and charm;
> Delightful eye and spirit – woodland farm,
> Long coastlines bordering waters far and near;
> Entrancing otter, gliding seaward here,
> Indents a valley beautiful and calm.
> Great cliffs to westward rise, but quite disarm
> Hostility to heights which some may fear.

Budleigh is still a favourite with contemporary players. John Walters claims that the sun always shines here. The view of the sea from some of the lawns is certainly inspiring though on a rare summer's day, the lawns can become baking hot. There are two pavilions. The first was built in 1870 but replaced some twenty years later. The 'new' pavilion was built in the Twenties and the bridge rooms added in 1930.

Budleigh Salterton Lawn Tennis and Croquet Club is a delightful place. Seated on the verandah of either pavilion, the hiss of the sea can be heard. There is also a nostalgic whiff of the colonial days of the Raj since the club has seen more than its fair share of 'crusty' characters. Budleigh is fortunate in having its own 'historian in residence', Dr Ralph Bucknall. He has constructed a complete record of the club's development from its beginning to 1970. His efforts trace Budleigh's slow metamorphosis from a Lawn Tennis club (ten courts and only four croquet lawns in 1919), to its present status as a croquet, bowls and bridge club. Along the way, he uncovered some fascinating tales of 'social warfare' amongst the members. 'There's an old rhyme that describes it all quite nicely' he says. 'It goes like this: The bluest of blue live in Budleigh but the women have faces like cod. The colonels talk only to generals and the generals talk only to God.'

Ralph Bucknall remembers how one lady, arriving for a tournament tea with a car full of cakes and jellies, asked another of the wives to come and help her unpack her load. The lady declined on the grounds that she was rather busy herself at that moment. Uproar broke out and letters were written to the club secretary during which it transpired that the main grievance was not that help had been 'refused' but that the command should never have been questioned as 'her husband is only a Major and mine is a Colonel!'

On another occasion, the military was itself the object of the combined outrage of the members. The club was taken over by the armed forces in 1940 (Budleigh even suffered a daylight bombing raid during the war in February of 1945) and members were enraged – not by the presence of the military but because some silly blighter amongst the visitors had managed to get jam on the bridge cards.

Ralph Bucknall remembers the dying days of tennis at Budleigh. 'We used to have three set matches, not five as at Wimbledon, and all the stars came here and spectators would queue for tickets. But as the game became more professional, the players demanded more money and the "gracious hospitality" that had been shown in the past began to disappear. It was such hard work to provide all the lunches and teas and the people who came were not as nice.' Sponsorship was also a problem. W. D. and H. O. Wills had provided the early funds but in the last days of tennis in the late Sixties there was no sponsorship and profits were falling fast.

Despite the withdrawal of the world of tennis, Budleigh still has an air of bustle about it. The club is host to several tournaments throughout the croquet season and the people are kindly and hospitable. Visitors are welcomed with much of the 'gracious hospitality' that Ralph Bucknall remembers and the little town itself is such a pretty place that an outing there becomes a delight on or off the croquet lawns. Arthur Lillie, describing Lily Gower's great victory at Budleigh in 1898, also paid tribute to this 'charming spot, with its red rocks and blue seas, its walks up the pretty river Otter bubbling with fine trout'. Very little has changed. Budleigh still represents a quiet oasis of calm. Sitting on the verandah of the new clubhouse, watching others at work in a game, hearing the satisfying clunk of croquet balls and the sound of the sea and smelling the burnt-out remains of Ralph Bucknall's pipe, makes for a very pleasant interlude in a frenetic world.

Bowdon in Cheshire is also renowned for its friendly atmosphere. Founded in 1911, the club has had a history of fluctuating fortunes. Between the wars, it benefited from the patronage of Lord Tollemache who, as a country member, came to offer coaching and, it seems, helped boost the membership to the point where the club was oversubscribed. Tollemache's annual house parties would also serve to swell the ranks of class players at Bowdon and his presence ensured that tournaments were eventful. However, during the Second World War the tournaments were cancelled and very little croquet was played at Bowdon. The club fell into a state of depression, unaided as it was by subsidies from any other sports club and continuing therefore on a very shaky financial basis. But continue it did and by the Seventies, it had finally struggled back to something of its old form. In 1973, Bowdon held its first official tournament since the war. A year later, it concentrated on wooing new members with social events such as Croquet suppers to which non-members were invited. A great deal of effort went into improving the lawns and coaching courses were held for beginners. All the activity seems to have paid off, for the membership increased, the club improved and in 1990, it hosted the prestigious President's Cup the main invitational event of the season.

Other clubs have struggled on through ups and downs like Bowdon. For example, Ipswich, founded in 1907 and Edgbaston, founded in 1919. The latter began a happy 'association' with the newly-formed

Stourbridge Club in the Seventies and an interesting account of the life of a small club appeared in the gazette in 1973. Stourbridge then did not even have a pavilion. Instead, it shared a small shed. Because of the shortage of lawns, (only two) double-banking (playing two games concurrently on the same lawn) was necessary but Stourbridge could not afford the second colour balls until its third season. After that, they seem to have managed to pack their courts to capacity as the writer proudly announced that 'there is a way of getting forty people on to two courts', an achievement which those club members fortunate enough to have many more lawns but still unhappy about 'sharing', would do well to remember.

In Southwick, the lawns seem to stretch out as far as the eye can see (there are eleven of them). It looks a fine club, set as it is, in a quiet part of Sussex by the sea, but it suffers from the occasional bout of inexplicable vandalism and for some players, the place always seems blighted by rain which makes the lawns slow. Others have recorded the 'warm, friendly atmosphere', the excellent food and the first-rate management of tournaments, especially in the days when Commander Giles Borrett was in control.

Further along the coast is Compton, compact, friendly and always sunny. According to the records books, a croquet club existed in Eastbourne as early as 1869 though little is known of its history except that it did not survive. The present club was founded by a local doctor with the teutonic name of Otto Holst. Two courts were rented from the Eastbourne Cricket and Football Club at the Saffrons, beginning a relationship which has lasted to the present day. The croquet club was called Compton after the home of the Dukes of Devonshire, Compton Place, which lay nearby. By 1902, there was a membership of eighty and a small waiting list. The club undoubtedly benefited from the influx of visitors to the annual end-of-season tournament at Devonshire Park and in 1906, a small pavilion was built. Other small clubs existed around the south coast in those days, including the Southdown Club at Lewes and the South Saxons at Hastings. Compton played matches against them all and in 1910, was narrowly defeated in the final of the inter-club championships when not one of its four men originally selected proved able to play. Among its notable members, it can count Lady Julian Parr, Women's Champion in 1913, Dudley Hamilton-Miller who played an active part on the Council and also in test matches, Handel Elvey and his wife Nora, Lord Tollemache and Cyril Tolley.

Lily Gower, Open champion in 1905, Women's champion three times,
Women's Gold Medallist and also, having entered and won the men's event in
1907, Men's Gold Medallist. She used a mallet with an unusually long handle
which she held with one hand at the top and the other almost halfway down
the shaft. Long skirts, hats and gloves have long since disappeared from the
wardrobe of the contemporary lady-champion.

C. L. O'Callaghan.

ABOVE C. L. O'Callaghan, drawn by H. F. Crowther Smith in 1929. The Irish player is illustrated in golfing dress. Crowther Smith entitled his picture 'Gone to Golf' and wrote 'to think Leslie likes that ugly pimply little white ball better than the pretty coloured ones'.

OPPOSITE Croquet 'style' often had as much to do with dress as with method of play. C. E. Willis (*top left*) had a style of play almost as 'peculiar' as his choice of footwear. Arthur Lillie wrote 'when aiming due north, he aims north-east' and complained that his style was half side and half front. Perhaps this was to compensate for the appalling condition of the lawns like the one pictured here. May Chester (*top right*) was a 'new style' player, swinging the mallet from the side rather than across the front. She won the Gold Medal in 1899. Ladies liked to pose in their finery but they almost certainly did not play in such preposterous hats, which would have prevented them from 'keeping the head down', essential when making a shot. Maud Drummond (*bottom left*) was Lady Champion in 1897 and was taught by her father Captain G. R. B. Drummond on their lawn in Petworth, Sussex. John Austin (*bottom right*) is shown here demonstrating his scythe-handled mallet and also a more 'relaxed' style of dress for gentlemen at the turn of the century.

Lord Tollemache's book *Croquet* published in 1914, was filled with self-portraits demonstrating how to make, for example a stop-shot take-off of medium length (*above left*), a cut rush (*above right*) and the correct finishing position of the hoop-running shot (*below*). Sneakers have long since replaced polished shoes.

D. D. Steel, shown sizing up a corner at Roehampton in 1937. A leading player at home and
abroad, she was a legend in her own lifetime.

Lady Julian Parr, poised to perform a roquet shot (*left*). She was later interviewed by the colourful Bryan Lloyd Pratt, shown here demonstrating his elegant side-swing and wearing his famous straw hat (*below left*). E. P. C. Cotter, (*bottom*) and the young John Solomon (*below*) were a formidable croquet partnership. They won the Doubles Championships nine times, (consecutively from 1961 to 1965).

Debbie Cornelius is one of Great Britain's (and the world's) contemporary leading lady players. Women are less evident in croquet today but when they do play, they tend to get right down to it.

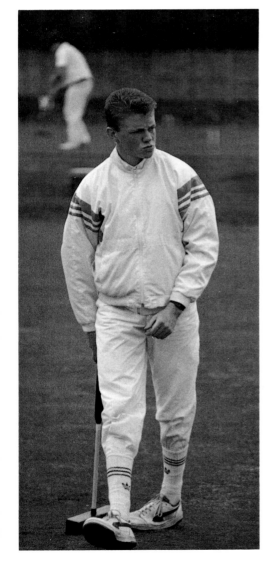

OPPOSITE Contemporary croquet is rich in champions. Keith Aiton (*top left*) was official coach to the Great Britain and Ireland Test Team in 1990, Mark Saurin (*bottom left*) never one to hide his feelings, started playing croquet at school. In 1988, he won the Men's Championship at the age of seventeen and two years later became the youngest member of the Test team. Richard Hilditch (*top right*) has always carried his weight in the croquet world, as has Stephen Mulliner (*bottom right*) author, player and current Chairman of the Croquet Association, here contemplating the O'Callaghan Cup which, to date, he has won four times at the South of England Championships.

The victorious 1990 Test Team of Great Britain and Ireland: Back row, left to right, Colin Irwin, William Prichard, Mark Saurin, Robert Fulford. Front row: Stephen Mulliner, David Openshaw (Captain), Mark Avery.

'Schools Croquet' has produced some fine players, not least Chris Clarke (*left*) winner of the President's Cup in 1988 and Robert Fulford (*below*) the World Champion in 1990.

ABOVE Spectators, particularly those who are also players, often take a serious view of events.

RIGHT Jerry Stark, of Arizona, USA, winner of the Fun Cup presented by the Italians to the 1989 World Championships.

Joe Hogan, New Zealand champion and one of the world's best players, lining up a shot during the first World Championships held at Hurlingham in 1989, which he won.

In 1959, the membership stood at sixty-five, the highest for twenty years but it was the late Sixties before fortunes really began to rise. By this time, Tolley had joined the club.

He was an amateur golf champion and he brought a certain amount of kudos to croquet at Compton. The club sailed into the Seventies. The pavilion was extended in 1972 and five silver cups which had languished, forgotten since 1940, were restored to the club by a local firm of solicitors. The membership slowly climbed towards the magic figure of ninety and as younger members joined, including Roger Wood, who led a small invasion from the Royal Observatory at Herstmonceaux, shorts were seen for the first time on the Compton lawns. Despite another slump in the mid-Eighties, the fortunes of the club remain high today. The membership hovers about the hundred mark and the club plays host to the South of England Championships each year. Roger Wood has proved indispensable on these occasions as tournament manager. Jake Moody has also contributed greatly but, perhaps the hardest worker is James Kellaway. As secretary and now chairman, he has steered Compton through many a patch of troubled water and his infectious enthusiasm has done much to help make Compton the happy place it now is.

It may not boast Budleigh's fine sea views or Southwick's grandeur but nothing can compete with Compton on a fine spring day. Then the daffodils are in bloom around the terraced lawns forming an L-shape in front of a smart wooden clubhouse. The trees, which in summer provide a pleasant spot to rest, are in leaf (though some were lost in the October storm of 1987) and the flat, well-kept lawns beckon. In May, it is always possible to imagine that this year, a handicap will plummet and success which has always seemed so difficult before, will come easily.

This is the hope of every club member and it is the members who keep the clubs alive. Much debate has raged in the croquet world over membership to the Croquet Association, the official body of the game. Some, wittingly or unwittingly echo Bryan Lloyd Pratt in calling for quality rather than quantity. They argue that an 'open to all-comers' policy overcrowds the clubs and lowers the standards. Others have felt that the game is 'too cheap' and that subscriptions and tournament fees should be increased. The days of rich benefactors and generous local councils seem long past and most clubs today recognize the need to live on their subscriptions and that the only way to do this, is to increase club membership. For many, the realization has long since dawned that if croquet is to thrive, it must be by means of a network of lively clubs which, in turn, means encouraging new membership.

Despite the low cost of equipment, croquet can still be a costly game for the young tournament player. He (or she) must pay his entry fee, the cost of his travel and often, the price of an hotel or boarding house for a night or two. Long gone are the days of luxury hotels catering lavishly for the elegant social life of the croquet player. Today's participant will more than likely find himself sharing a room in a small seaside boarding house and counting the cost of a few drinks at the pub in the evening.

Some clubs have made an attempt to encourage players to their tournaments by researching lists of recommended hotels and making clubs' premises available for evening snacks, or providing a list of members who are happy to offer accommodation to visitors for a night or two. Unfortunately, generous assistance like this is limited, not least because those who work so hard to support the clubs through a busy season of tournaments already find themselves overstretched with administrative chores.

The clubs form the backbone of croquet, without which, it could not survive and there is no doubt that since the Second World War it is only voluntary hard work which has kept many of the clubs in existence. Throughout the length and breadth of England, croquet boasts armies of unsung heroes and heroines who give up free time to manage tournaments, to offer coaching to beginners, to bake cakes and brew tea to feed hungry players, and to clear away and wash up the whole show afterwards. In the process, they keep croquet alive and continue its worthwhile tradition as a happy, social affair.

THE ETIQUETTE
Dress, Behaviour and Style

'P lenty of people are prepared to go through life in a humdrum manner, altogether without style, and are comparatively colourless, uninteresting specimens of humanity. Just so with croquet. You may even be blessed with eye enough to make a good shot, an angelic temper, plenty of pluck, and a fair amount of luck, and yet, without definite style, you will never belong to "Class A".'

When Lt.-Col. the Honourable Henry Needham wrote these words in 1901, he was referring to the method of play. He called it 'attitude' and his use of the word nicely encompassed all the elements of style, etiquette and dress.

Then as now, the Laws of Croquet made no regulations for dress, though in 1899, it was stated under the regulations for prize meetings, 'That every competitor shall wear tennis shoes if called upon'. Today, the annually published Fixtures List, under the heading of General Conditions and Information, insists that flat shoes must be worn on the lawns and recommends 'predominantly white clothing'.

Tennis shoes and whites have become almost 'de rigeur' for tournaments and though nothing in the regulations forbids it, it is increasingly rare to see a competitor in bright colours. Some compromise with cream. Many add touches of an individual nature. Bryan Lloyd Pratt, Humphrey Hicks, Richard Hilditch have all, at some time or another, favoured a hat. Leslie Riggall has gone to great lengths to defend the white trilby, pointing out that Lord Tollemache had generally worn one, as had some of the Irish players who dominated the game in the Twenties. He confessed he found a cap more comfortable himself but in any case, the South African sun which threatened the unwary with skin cancer, required a player to seek protection under a wide-brimmed hat.

In Riggall's opinion, the wearing of whites is a 'mark of respect for the game'. Others felt that players dressed in white, 'like enterprising play, help to make croquet more attractive to the spectator'.

Whatever the rationale, the question of correct dress, as also the subject of etiquette, has preoccupied English players throughout the history of the game. In the earliest days, red boots were sometimes fashionable for the ladies. These were worn under voluminous crinoline skirts, which were in turn, kept under control by huge wire hoops. In an essay in Arthur Lillie's *Croquet Up to Date*, Miss Kathleen Waldron describes these 'glorious days of the crinoline, when ladies wore the ingenious anti-Aeolian at croquet or archery – a sort of wire cage to keep voluminous skirts in trim'. The upper skirt was often looped up with a small chain but the whole affair must have severely restricted movement and been excruciatingly uncomfortable. The only advantage of such an ensemble was that it enabled the ladies to indulge in a little light cheating. At least, much reference has been made by successive writers to the surreptitious shifting of a ball undercover of a skirt to a better position in front of a hoop.

With croquet's rise in popularity, croquet accessories became all the rage. *The Queen* newspaper recorded in 1865 the trend towards this 'ornamental jewellery. You may see pencil cases it is said in the shape of croquet mallets, a game of croquet on sash buckles and an ingenious little brooch formed of a gold mallet from which is suspended by a little chain, a croquet ball.'

With the end of the Victorian era and the advent of the Edwardians, volume seems to have gone from a lady's skirt to her head. Dress remained long, and looked both pretty and elegant, but ladies posed in studios and on croquet lawns in vast hats which seemed hideously precarious and could hardly have been worn in serious competition for they would have prevented a player from successfully keeping her 'head down' – all important when hitting a single ball.

Even in more relaxed dress, of skirt and blouse topped by a moderate straw hat, the Edwardian ladies were an inspiring sight. The men were less so. Much discussion seems to have taken place as to the 'correct dress' for them on the lawns. Some men played in their shirt sleeves, others posed in rather natty suits. One commentator thought it 'out of character to "sport" a "blazer" or any garment suggestive of a change of attire. The happy medium exists in the usual English costume – off parade so to speak – of a quiet suit of serge or tweed, or in great heat, of nankeen or equally cool material.'

The gazettes of the Twenties carry advertisements for flat overshoes which ladies could wear with the then popular flapper-style footwear which had a high heel. These 'croquet soles' were advertised as available in black, brown and white and 'approved by most of the croquet managers'. They strapped onto the feet over the shoe and looked very strange and uncomfortable.

The 'quiet suit' seems to have sufficed for some until after the wars. Players then began to 'sport' blazers for Test matches and these events gave new fuel to the debate on what to wear. The 1950 Test tour convinced the British players that, in matters of sartorial elegance and also of comportment, they had something to learn from the antipodes. Dudley Hamilton-Miller, who captained the 1950 team, paid tribute to the 'impeccable manners' of the New Zealand spectators, while two of the players, John Solomon and Humphrey Hicks, commented on the contrast between the smart appearance of the players in the southern hemisphere when compared with the 'slovenly' state of some of those back home. Their letter prompted an editorial note on the question of suitable attire, which suggested that the New Zealanders at least, had always taken a particular interest in dress. The editor quoted from a copy of the *New Zealand Croquet Gazette* which described how a Mrs Duncan, a bank manager's wife, was wont to select her croquet teams not on playing ability, but according to their dress. 'Many were the heartburnings of those who remained at home because their trains lacked sufficient length or their hats the necessary number of plumes.'

In a croquet book he published in the mid-Fifties, Maurice Reckitt added a note on costume in which he quoted the then requirements for tournament play, 'such flat-soled boots or shoes as cannot damage the court' and recommended rainwear, most practically, of the kind worn by golfers. Men looked best in flannels, he thought, while ladies were advised to remember that croquet is a sport and so 'sports clothes are those most appropriate to it; "garden party dresses" are not'.

By the Sixties, most players in England had taken to playing in whites for competitions but the question of 'correct' dress still remained unanswered. 'Rover', the regular column of the gazette, complained in 1965 that, 'Far too many players still appear at tournaments looking as though they are on their way to paint a boat'. This was the era of 'Lloyd Pratt Straws' and casual cravats knotted at the throat à la Noël Coward. Others felt that wet weather made wearing whites ridiculous. In any case, the days of flannels and pleated skirts, 'bowls style' were on the way out. Today, Nigel Aspinall (whose only concession to modern sportswear appears to be a thin waterproof jacket) probably marks the end of the era that played in long trousers. Shorts have taken over.

In 1975, David Openshaw, later Captain of the British Test team, made his initial appearance at Hurlingham dressed in what one eye-witness described as 'boy scout buff-coloured shorts'. It was the beginning of the end. (Though there are those who contend that Richard Rothwell started the downturn by wearing shorts as early as the mid-Fifties.) The current generation of top players, for the most part, turn out dressed like tennis players, some complete with the sort of logo-ed accessories (wristbands and the like) that are the commercial badges of croquet's great sporting rival. Rain does little to dampen the enthusiasim for this skimpy clothing which is occasionally covered with some sort of light waterproof.

A letter to the November 1985 edition of the gazette, asked for help on the right sort of waterproofing, suggesting that cyclists, walkers or climbers might share their wisdom on the subject. The letter appeared in the edition which carried a photograph on its cover of two young women posing beside the peg dressed extremely smartly. The following edition offered two useful suggestions on brands of water-proof clothing (which did not cause condensation) and carried a letter hooting derisively at the two 'exquisitely dressed' young ladies, one of whom it seemed was wearing shoes with heels.

Today's young players rarely bother with elegance, inappropriate or otherwise. Reporting on a championship match in the *Financial Times* a few years ago, the writer felt moved to comment in some detail on the sort of 'slovenly' manner that had been so decried in the Fifties. One player wore white boxing boots, another displayed his stomach through the gap between shorts and crumpled T-shirt, a third had forgotten to shave. The one consolation to those who, in the Fifties, had urged the English players to follow the New Zealand and

Australian example and 'adopt a uniform' is that however short the shorts (for ladies now as well as men) or relaxed the T-shirt, it is at least, more often than not, in some concessionary 'shade' of white.

During the first World Championship singles held at Hurlingham, the New Zealanders and Australians appeared in long shorts, long socks and bushhats, looking like refugees from the forces of the Second World War. The Americans added another dimension to the subject of dress with Jerry Stark's jolly red braces. But what might have appeared to be a new fashion was only an old one making another appearance, as braces had been seen about the hoops before. An editorial in the June gazette of 1951, commented that no longer did men play without waistcoat or jacket, having learnt that spectators were unimpressed by the sight, 'however beautiful, their expensive Bond Street braces may be'.

Contrary to the fears expressed down the ages, various styles of dress have had little effect on the nature of the game. It may be that a man appearing to play dressed as if he had 'just emerged from his potting shed', could cause a degree of comment in the gazette but the reflection on the game itself is hardly likely to be significant. No more say, than if Steve Davis had suddenly taken to playing snooker in shorts. Without doubt, the occurence would raise a few eyebrows but one wonders if it would really diminish admiration for playing skill. Far more important than dress, is the question of behaviour.

Here too it would seem the British players have something to learn from the New Zealanders. Dudley Hamilton-Miller's comment on the impeccable manner of the spectators in New Zealand in the Fifties would be hard to match in England. Most spectators are croquet players and most croquet players find it hard to refrain from commenting on how they would have played a particular shot – or how they would play the next one.

Maurice Reckitt was famous for his loud 'asides' but he was certainly not alone in this. Long before Mr Reckitt's day there were unofficial commentaries on the game, for one writer advised gently 'it is best to believe unfriendly remarks to be made in the heat of uncontrolled excitement'. Many croquet games are still played to the accompaniment of a Greek Chorus in the wings for no-one can play so well, or be so tactically brilliant as the man on the sidelines.

The Official Rules of the United States Croquet Association (1983–4 edition) make specific reference to this subject and state: 'Spectators should abstain from audible comments on the game'. They would doubtless be surprised at the amount of audible comment surrounding a tournament in England, as indeed are the New Zealand players who regard 'off the lawn comment' as a sign of disrespect. The Laws of association croquet state that a player may talk to his opponent. Indeed, he is 'entitled to ask his adversary about the state of the game at all times'. He can also consult his opponent if he suspects that he is about to play a 'questionable' stroke. Should their opinions differ as to whether or not a ball has been hit or moved, 'the positive opinion is generally to be preferred to the negative'. However, a player 'is not entitled to receive advice from anyone'.

Much debate took place at the start of the century as to whether or not one should comment if an adversary played a wrong ball or committed another kind of foul. Etiquette, then, as now, was a 'troublesome question' but one player felt that most situations could be remedied in the following way. 'If I see my adversary likely to make a break, (I) sit down beside someone I know, talk, and take a general interest in the game, but always leave it to the player to mention it if he has made a foul of that kind.'

In recent years, two other practices which seem quite ordinary in other spheres of life have provoked a surprising amount of debate in association croquet circles. To many, shaking hands after a game seems a perfectly natural action, signalling mutual thanks for a good game, appreciation of the loser, congratulations to the winner and a small concession to emotional relief that the match is over. Others of a less demonstrative nature consider any kind of physical contact in croquet unnecessary. In a protracted paragraph on the subject in a 1984 copy of the gazette, one debater began by saying that he could not recall ever shaking hands with his opponent at the end of a game and went on to observe that his usual practice was to 'raise my arm to my opponent when pegging out'.

It is unlikely that croquet players will ever throw themselves at each other like footballers or cricketers or fall to their knees in public prayer as do some tennis players. Shaking hands seems very tame by comparison.

Another custom hovering on the edge of acceptance into croquet lore, is the buying of drinks for the loser. Some older players have occasionally found the exchange of rounds of liquid refreshment after a morning's play 'unnatural'. The only reasoning to be found for this lies in the thought that the 'unnaturalness' of alcohol in the morning derives from an ingrained respect for a kind of colonial timetable for cocktails and snifters with strict rules related to sundown. One croquet player who boasted that in the mid-Fifties when he was particularly 'active on the courts and won more games than lost' and could not recall ever consoling his opponent with a glass, relates how having been 'comprehensively beaten by a teenager just after three o'clock' he felt obliged to turn down the young man's offer of a drink. In croquet, as in much of life, timing is everything.

In 1926, a Miss 'E L' in an article entitled 'The Mentality of Croquet Players', declared somewhat starkly that 'Croquet players do not like each other'. Her article went on to puzzle over the fact that, given this mutual disapprobation, so many of them then proceeded to marry their opponents. Where did they find the time she mused, preoccupied to the point of obsession with their game as they so often were, to ask or indeed answer the question, 'Will you marry me?' More perplexing still was why they married. Needless to say, useful answers were not forthcoming. Yet croquet does have a good record of playing 'couples', the Beatons, the Elveys and the Longmans among them.

Willy Longman met his wife in 1930 when she was a mere beginner, and having partnered her to success through the handicap doubles, soon became engaged to her and married a few months later. The event 'produced one of the most notable alliances our game has known'. Perhaps, like bridge, good croquet partners rely on sound combination. Certainly there are few more gracious occurrences than that of a good player, guiding a willing beginner through a game. The very best are those who manage to make the lesser player feel that they are contributing substantially while actually doing the work for them. At such times, croquet provides a model of gallantry and good manners (and supreme patience). At others, indifference, despondency and disgust cast clouds across the sunniest nature and 'etiquette' becomes mere idealism.

How should a player conduct himself in croquet? In 1961, an article on the subject, signed simply by 'A. Player', offered, in essence, the following advice:

'Always adopt a sportsmanlike attitude to your opponent; enjoy a game whether winning or losing, say "thank-you" at the end of a game and if you are the loser walk quietly away, if the winner, collect the clips and balls, leave the lawn ready for the next players and report your success to the tournament manager. Be punctual for games. Don't talk to spectators when you are the out-player. Always vacate the court when you are not playing and stand or sit out of your opponent's line of shot. Watch your opponent and think ahead so that when his turn is over you can commence play quickly. Don't make comments on your play (or your opponent's) during the game and make sure you know the laws as, for the most part, players act as their own referees.'

It seems a pretty comprehensive outline but perhaps the most important point for tournament play is to get on with the game. Nigel Aspinall, well known for his speed about the court, has always disliked what he calls 'statues', those players who begin their turn by taking up a position in the centre of the court and stand still while they wonder what to do next. He shares this enthusiasm for action with Walter Peel, who more than a century ago would cry, 'For goodness sake do something! Better decide at once wrongly than waste time in hesitation.'

Most top players will have watched their opponent closely enough to anticipate his next few moves. They are therefore prepared to quickly follow on with the game once they take the innings.

To date, British croquet has few non-playing spectators but should a spectator stray into a game, there are a few important points to remember. Keep off the lawns and out of a player's line of sight. If it is necessary to move past him, do so when he is not actually making a shot and go quietly. Applause can be appreciated for a particularly fine shot but most player-spectators restrict themselves to a subdued cry of 'good hoop!' or similar. Dress, (apart from regulation flat-soled shoes) is nowadays more a matter of personal preference but women who insist on turning up in long skirts in imitation of a more 'elegant' era will find it near impossible to play the modern centre-style and everyone would do well to avoid any kind of clothing which flaps about because it can inhibit a player's swing.

'Style' in croquet means technique. As such, there seem to be as many different 'styles' as there are players in the game. Historical precedent exists for this observation. In 1900, Claude Heneage wrote 'No croquet enthusiast can fail to be struck by the diversity of style in playing the game adopted by the best players . . . It is perhaps owing to the fact that no perfect recognized style exists that consistent good form is so rare; in fact, it is no unusual occurrence for a first-class player to win one game in the most brilliant form, and to be completely off his game in the next.' The same applies today.

Technically, style generally refers to the stance, grip and swing of a player and these are discussed in detail below but 'style' is also interpretative and often an individual expression of prevailing fashion. Some players feel that croquet style is so indicative that they can tell a competitor from a distance simply by his body movements. But unlike tennis or golf where a player can usually learn his style, in croquet, most success seems to lie in doing what comes naturally. This may be a result of the fact that many of the top players started when they were young. In this way, they developed 'styles' to suit their particular needs at the time.

The most famous example of this is John Solomon, who, as a child, was too small to hold a mallet in any sort of orthodox fashion and simply gripped the shaft with both hands, as one might hold on to a pole. He went on to play like this (though not all the time, he frequently changed his grip according to the shots) and thereby created the 'Solomon grip'. The way a player holds the mallet is probably the first thing he discovers about the game so it seems wise to start with the subject.

The grip: There are several different ways of holding a mallet but, within reason, the one that is right is the one which the player finds most comfortable. Those most frequently in use are the Solomon grip, described above, where both hands hold the mallet at the top of the shaft, the standard grip, and the Irish grip.

The standard grip holds the mallet shaft at the top with one hand (usually the left if the player is right-handed) and about six inches further down with the other. The fingers of the top hand curl round the mallet shaft and the thumb either rests on top or lies round against the side nearest the body. The palm of the other hand faces forward and is used to 'push' the mallet into the swing. Many players hold the index finger straight down the centre of the back of the shaft (the side nearest to the body) but each individual must find what is most comfortable.

In the Irish grip (so called because it was used by some of the Irish players of the Twenties, notably 'Duff' Mathews), the hands are more or less in the same position on the mallet but both palms face forward. Nigel Aspinall and Mark Avery use this grip. Both players are distinguished for the rhythm of their swing and the subsequent accuracy of their shooting and it may be that this method of holding the mallet enables a reasonably tall man (as is the case with these two men) to get better control of the pendulum effect of the mallet. There is no doubt that a person's height also has some bearing on the matter as does the weight of the mallet head (see next chapter).

Having established the most comfortable method of holding the mallet, the player should then decide on his style and stance. 'Style' in this case means either playing with the mallet held to the side of the body (known, obviously enough as side-style) or with the mallet swinging between the legs, (centre-style). The latter is by far the most common today. It requires a degree of strength in the wrists but offers more accuracy in the line of shot.

Centre-style can be played either with the feet placed parallel, or by adopting a stance where one foot is placed slightly before the other. Some players, especially in New Zealand, keep the feet remarkably close together. This can lead to a painful clunk on the ankle if the swing of the mallet is not totally accurate. To stand with the feet too far apart is uncomfortable (and puts some strain on the lower back when bending into the swing). Once again, the player must experiment until he finds the fashion that best suits him.

Side-style requires the feet to be one in front of the other, usually with most of the weight on the forward foot. The shoulders should be at right angles to the mallet when it is swung. Certain croquet shots necessitate this 'side-style'. The roll shot, for example, used to drive the balls across the court at relatively the same distance requires the player to stand much further forward with the feet level with the balls and the shaft of the mallet held much lower down to gain greater control over the stroke.

Side-style as described here, was once called 'front-style' while, just to confuse the matter further, side-style then referred to hitting the ball across the front of the body as in golf or cricket. Much debate on which was better took place at the beginning of the century, 'front-style' having been introduced by B. C. Evelegh, Open Champion in the 1870s. Arthur Lillie held a sort of poll among the top players of the day. Some, like Captain Drummond came down firmly in favour of what was then 'side-style' and was the more traditional of the two methods (and had once been played using only one hand). Others, like Mr C. E. Willis, felt that 'any style of play is correct, for it is not the position but the man behind the mallet that tells'. Maud Drummond, Lily Gower and May Chester were among the early lady champions to play 'front-style'. Others continued to prefer the front-style until comparatively recently. Maurice Reckitt has a photograph demonstrating this method of play in his book *Croquet Today* (Macdonald 1954). The player stands with his feet almost together and seems to be holding the mallet very near the top of the shaft, rather like a golfer about to swing a putt. This method is certainly rare now and modern textbooks only describe the two methods outlined above. Of these, lady players still sometimes prefer the side-style as being more elegant and less restricted by a longish skirt but most younger women overcome the impediment of dress by playing in shorts or trousers, and like their male contemporaries, favour the centre-style.

Lord Tollemache advocated bending the knees when swinging the mallet so as to 'sit down' on a shot. Quite often today, a player can be seen springily bending into his swing before making the shot, rather like a skier flexing for a jump. Others, like contemporary champion Stephen Mulliner, simply 'address' the ball, then hit it. Maurice Reckitt gives the subject a lengthy chapter, interspersed with a great many demonstrational photographs. In the end, too much reflection can leave a person paralysed. After all is said and done, the object is to hit the ball squarely. However one does it, it is very much a matter of personal experimentation.

Even so, most modern experts advise the player to relax and bend the knees and to stand with eyes focused on the back of the ball when first 'addressing' it. Rest the base of the mallet lightly on the ground with its centre just a half inch or so behind the centre of the ball which in turn should be a foot or so from the feet. Keep the head still and down, (eyes on the ball) then swing the mallet through in a half circle, pushing through with the upper arms so that the movement ends with arms extended, though not stiff.

Played well, croquet is a supremely elegant game. There is a rhythm to the long strokes and a delicacy to the precision shots of a top-class player that are a delight to watch. In general, the ambience of the game is still gracious and relaxing and most croquet players are friendly and welcoming to newcomers to their sport. Whether played to win at tournament level, or played for fun to the civilized accompaniment of tea and polite conversation, croquet is hard to beat.

THE EQUIPMENT
Mallets Old and New

T he shape and size of today's mallets are pretty standard but it was not always so. The earliest mallets were made from a variety of materials and came in many forms. Those first descended from the game of pall mall, were usually made of ash or boxwood and had tiny curved heads which often weighed less than the ball. They could be wielded (the practice seems to have been to strike the ball rather as a polo player swings his stick) with one or both hands.

When play first became 'organized' in the 1860s, mallets were flat, cylindrical, heavy, light, large and small. Arguments were offered in favour of all. A heavy mallet for example, was considered best for rolls, splits and take-offs as it required less wrist action. J. H. Hale, a founder member of the All England Croquet Club committee, introduced the 'Cavendish', a heavy mallet with a lignum vitae head. It particularly suited his style of play – he was also a cricketer and liked hard hitting. In contrast, Walter Jones Whitmore preferred the smaller, lighter mallet which suited a more precise style of play. The light mallet was also considered better for the three-ball break and for taking position around the hoops.

To begin with, there was nothing to stop a player from using a variety of mallets, both light and heavy, during the same game. Soon however, this practice was forbidden. Prichard writes that a new rule was introduced because one player, the Honourable Arthur Capell kept a tiny mallet tucked into his waistcoat which he used to get his ball safely through the hoop. Be that as it may, in 1899 it was laid down that both ends of the mallet head should be parallel and the same size and shape. This disposed of certain oddities like the wedge-shaped mallet and another with one rounded and one flat end. Some of these had been cunningly designed to secure advantage on the lawns. For example, a mallet with one face at a sharp receding angle, enabled the player to 'scoop' out the ball when it was wired.

In 1911 it was ruled that a mallet could not be changed more than once in a game (unless damaged) and the law was not modified until 1947 when the present law, that a mallet should not be changed during a turn, was introduced.

A popular style at the end of the last century was the 'sliced' mallet, introduced by Walter Peel. This mallet was made by shaving off a section of the head on the side nearest the ground. It was taken up by many players, some of whom went so far as to have their mallets 'plated' with a brass plate screwed to the bottom. This considerably 'weighted' the mallet and required less exertion on certain strokes, though it made it almost impossible to play delicate ones.

The idea of the sliced mallet was to get the point of impact into the centre of the mallet's face but the fashion began to lose favour when it became obvious that there were other ways of achieving this – for example by simply reducing the circumference of the mallet head.

Cassell's *Book of Sports and Pastimes* in 1896 gave a long description of the various kinds of mallets of the day, including a variety with a 'looking glass' fitted which enabled the player to see the ball at which he was aiming reflected in it.

Mallet shafts were also various. Cassell described one shaped at the top like a spade handle with a shaft tightly bound with whipcord and leather and with two thin pieces of iron connecting the wooden shaft with the mallet head. 'The owner of this machine, when about to strike, grasped the spade with his left hand, with his knuckles turned towards the striking end, and steadied the handle by laying hold of the whipcord. It required a most inelegant attitude to perform properly with it, as the player had to stoop completely over the balls and turn his head askew to take aim.' And people think that Lewis Carroll's description of trying to play with a flamingo was mere fancy!

There were mallets with octagonal handles, round or square handles, some smooth, some rasped, some wrapped like golf clubs, others bound like bats, some covered with cork and others with gutta percha. A certain Mr Austin of Maidstone who was a 'front' player, introduced a 'scythe-handled mallet'. (The same gentleman invented a kind of 'stay' to hold hoops more firmly in the ground. It was known as 'Austin's Holdfast'.) Arthur Lillie had a great collection of mallets. W. W. Bruce, Gold Medallist in the late 1890s, wrote that, 'Their name is legion. He has them about twenty inches long in the head; very short, about four inches; some with bits of lead that you can take out and put according to the stroke you have to play; some with India-rubber ends; some with cork; but with them all he is equally dangerous.'

Bruce also described some of the other preferences of the day. Mr Bonham-Carter, for instance, played 'with a clumsy black mallet which must weigh about 6 lbs, with no spring, and as unlikely-looking an instrument as one can imagine'. Mr Trevor Williams played with a 'little yellow mallet weighing about 2½ lbs'. Others managed to work wonders on the lawns with mallets that were obviously peculiar to their own talents. Mr Heneage's had a warped handle, Mr Willis' mallet was 'all broken at the head' and Lord Doneraile's was hard to describe 'but if you cut about ten inches off a common cart-wheel, and then used the spoke as a handle, you would get something like it'.

The commonest type of mallet in Lillie's day was a plain cylindrical shape made of boxwood. It was eight to ten inches in length and had a diameter of some three inches, sometimes less. The handle was made of ash and was two feet, eight inches long. As this was the era of the 'sequence game' (balls were played in order of colour), some players had the colours of the proper order painted on the stem of the mallet.

Another fashion, of which Lillie heartily approved, was to face one end of the mallet head with a slice of India rubber, an inch in thickness. This was originally introduced to help players make long, difficult strokes as the India rubber gave extra impetus to the ball. But it was soon discovered that the modification also helped to better perform roll strokes, hoop running and peeling, and in addition, 'muffled' the sound of any double tapping. No wonder it became the rage.

The purists argued strongly against such an aid to the game and in 1901 they succeeded in having India rubber ends banned.

Manufacturers, it seems, were happy to make mallets to any specification. There were the wooden variety, made of greenheart, rock elm and ash but there were also those made of grander materials.

At least two people had ivory mallets, Sir John Lawrence, a viceroy of India and the Countess of Cavan.

John Jaques, whose grandfather, Thomas, had started the business in 1795 as a bone and ivory turner, advocated turkey boxwood for croquet balls. 'It possesses strength and elasticity, great durability and is of the proper specific gravity'. His firm produced many other kinds of games some of which sound quite ingenious. One was The Snake and Bird Puzzle which was played with 'a beautifully gilden snake'. The 'bird' was placed in the centre of the table and the tail of the snake in any position of the players' choice two feet from the edge. The puzzle consisted of placing several pieces of snake together so as to get the bird, or any part of it within the snake's mouth. 'Upwards of a thousand combinations may be made without violating these conditions and when completed the snake, by its graceful curves, forms a beautiful object on the table.' Another intriguing game was 'Geographical Loto' played on 'twelve beautiful maps'. 'Happy Families' was introduced to England by Jaques and the original Mr Bung the Brewer, Mr Pots the Painter and so on were drawn by Tenniel, who was then the chief cartoonist of *Punch*. Jaques also invented snakes and ladders, ludo and tiddlywinks but their name is probably most closely linked with croquet. Even so they had several strong rivals when croquet first appeared as an organized game.

They included Slazenger in Cannon Street, Parkins and Gotto's in Oxford Street and F. H. Ayers of Aldergate. The latter helped Arthur Lillie design a 'double-weight mallet' which had a removable weight fastened round the head of the mallet handle. In general, the length of these mallets was around two foot, ten inches. Some were shorter, others about a metre in length. In 1863, a box of eight ash mallets, balls, hoops, starting posts, clips and rules cost fifteen shillings.

Several companies which had already established themselves in other sports also tried to accommodate the public's new enthusiasm for the game. James Buchanan of Piccadilly, Archery Manufacturers by appointment to the Royal Family and to the Emperors of Russia and Brazil, introduced mallets made of the Canadian rock elm they used in bow-making, recommending that it had great 'spring and elasticity' and as such, was superior to ash. They were certainly very expensive, costing from twenty guineas upwards.

Other manufacturers made use of the croquet boom to promote sales of fencing, tents, flags, macassar oil, and most notably, seats. Garden seats were produced in every possible style, particularly by a Mr Green of Bond Street who also invented croquet shades.

Choosing a mallet, then as now, was very much a matter of individual taste. Some preferred a springy shaft, others a rigid handle. Some years later, the Reverend Elvey (who made his own mallets) took up the subject.

'A mallet to a croquet player is just as important as his bag of clubs to a golfer, or his cue to a billiard player,' he wrote. Although individual preference undoubtedly played an important part in the selection process, Elvey felt that there were certain characteristics that every good mallet should have.

The shaft, for example, should be straight. On this matter, he was adamant, pointing out that if the shaft was not straight, the player was unlikely to hit straight. Elvey preferred a plain shaft without a binding, as it could be washed clean with a sponge and water. Crowther-Smith agreed, feeling that plain wood, with no decoration, contributed 'to the important matter of touch'. He advocated a very whippy shaft for hoop running and pass rolls but as he wrote some years later, Maurice Reckitt felt that a very springy shaft was likely to 'take charge' of the player and was not therefore recommended for the beginner.

The head should be heavy enough to do its job but light enough for the player to control it, in other words, well-balanced for the style of the player. Balance of course, was a matter of weight. Some players, like Cyril Corbally and before him, John Hale, liked a heavy mallet. This meant a slower stroke which in turn, could conflict with a player's timing. The Australians tended to favour lighter mallets in which the lack of weight was compensated for by elasticity in the shaft.

By this time, boxwood had become expensive. Satinwood was tried as an alternative but was liable to split. Lignum vitae, heavy and hard, seemed the best alternative, though as it tended to split at the edges, it was advisable to have them bound with brass. The shaft was usually made of hickory with various kinds of grip – cork, rubber, artificial leather or even string. Heavy mallets had gradually given way to lighter ones as the range narrowed to between two pounds, fourteen ounces and three and a half pounds.

Today, there are still no limits on weight or size of mallet, though the laws now require that the end faces should be matching and made of wood 'or any other non-metallic material provided that no playing advantage is gained over wood'.

As woods like lignum vitae become rare, more mallets are made in the rectangular shape which wastes less wood in the manufacturing process than the cylindrical form. Some are marked with a line, or spot, to help assist the player in taking accurate aim. Others are bound at the ends to protect the faces. Contemporary players experiment as much as their forefathers to discover the best weight and style for themselves. Champion player, Stephen Mulliner, likes a larger than average head, another tournament player has adopted a home-made one-design aluminium construction which, though faced with wood, in keeping with the laws, nonetheless makes an unattractive metallic clank each time it strikes the ball.

The rule for new players must be to try before you buy. Clubs are good places to find a selection of second-hand mallets and by playing with mallets of different weights and lengths, the novice can soon discover which suits him best. The selection will depend on personal height, strength of wrists and style of play. There is no 'right' shape, size or weight and as Maurice Reckitt observed, the only real criteria is to 'choose your mallet, do not let your mallet choose you'.

Once chosen, providing it is given a modicum of care, a mallet can last some time. W. W. Bruce, inherited a mallet from a friend in India. It was so 'rickety that the head and handle are apt to show signs of parting company. It's owner "gives it a drink" – in other words, "holds it in the water-butt" after which it apparently recovers.'

More conventional care simply consists of wiping the mallet clean after play and storing it head upwards, preferably in a rack or a stand. Resting the mallet head on the floor with the shaft at an angle against a wall can encourage the shaft to warp.

In 1900, Lt.-Col. Needham gave some advice on mallet care which seems as pertinent today as it did then. He wrote:

'Good mallets, like good guns, rods, bats, cues or racquets, are worthy of being really taken care of, wiped dry and clean after play, kept in a proper place and oiled when laid aside out of season. Careless folk leave them out in blistering sun or soaking rain, or all night on a wet lawn, pile heavy articles across the handles, knock pegs and hoops in with the heads and even hurl them like knobkerries at a flying cat.'

Contemporary mallets tend to be too expensive for such wild behaviour. A good one will cost in the region of fifty pounds while a 'Rolls-Royce' model can be more than double that price. Some of today's top players have had mallets named after them, Jaques' brass-bound 'Solomon' mallet for example, or Townsend's 'Aspinall'. Other players have gone into production themselves, either as designers or as manufactures. Jackson mallets, made by the New Zealand champion, are one of the most attractive in both appearance and price and can be ordered from England. At the other end of the spectrum are those mallets produced on a very small scale. Players Colin Irwin, Martin French and Stuart Packer have all produced their own mallet heads some of which have provided models for other would-be inventors.

Once he has a mallet, the keen amateur will make best progress by joining a club as here he will find all the other paraphernalia of croquet. This includes hoops, balls, peg, clips, corner flags, corner pegs, baulk-line markers, check fences and a court.

Until 1870, the court could be of almost any size. Walter Jones Whitmore suggested maximum dimensions of a hundred yards in length by ten yards wide – just about big enough to park a jumbo jet. In 1871, the size was standardized to a more modest forty yards by thirty and was further reduced some half dozen years later to thirty-five yards by twenty-eight, which remain the full-size court's dimensions today.

Hoops have greatly diminished in size since the early days of croquet. Once vast round objects, fixed in 'huge oaken sockets', they are now made of metal which is five-eighths of an inch in diameter and painted white. (Blue was the recommended colour for the early variety but this was later changed to 'white or French grey'.) They stand twelve inches from ground to crown and the parallels should not be more than four inches apart (in championship play, they can be narrowed to three and eleven sixteenths of an inch). The crown of the starting hoop is painted blue, while that of the rover hoop is painted red. To 'make' a hoop, a ball must have passed far enough through it for a mallet head to slide down the side of entry without touching the ball.

Balls have always been spherical. In the 1860s, the correct circumference was ten inches, they usually came in sets of eight (one for each mallet) and were made from a variety of woods. Captain Mayne Reid had a preference for light chestnut or sycamore. He found the 'heart-wood of an old (sycamore) tree' the best material and recommended that the balls be painted in a combination of colours. 'The more vivid the colour, the prettier will be the effect on the greensward and the pleasanter the play.' Balls were then not usually coloured all over but painted in stripes.

Lt.-Col. Needham felt that, 'No one should play with any balls other than the regulation boxwood ones, viz three and five eighths of an inch in diameter (the standard size from about 1870 onwards) weight not less than 14½ ounces, or more than 15½ ounces . . . painted in plain colours, blue, red, black and yellow.' By the early 1900s, the old style of painting balls in stripes was obsolete. Some disliked them for aesthetic reasons, others because they reasoned that the painted variety actually kept better as the paint had a compressing, binding effect. For the same reason, the balls became pitted, rather like golf balls, as they held the paint better. Trials were already being carried out with composition balls by the beginning of the century. In America, wood had already been abandoned in favour of hard rubber. Composition was welcomed because it offered uniformity of weight and size and did not chip. Already, the 'standard' ball had been determined – painted, pitted, good on fast lawns with plenty of side and follow but with a tendency to 'drag' on wet lawns, made of composite and three and five-eighths of an inch in diameter.

The size of the present balls is the same, 'plus or minus one thirty-second of an inch'. They are also the same colours, but the alternate colours of green, brown, pink and white (part of the original set of eight) are also permitted and are often used when players are 'double banking' or playing two games simultaneously on the same court. The old sequence game required that balls be played in order: Blue, red, black and yellow. This is no longer the case, but once a striker has begun a turn with one of his two colours, he cannot play the partner ball – no matter how many hoops he may have run.

After the toss at the beginning of a game, the winner is allowed to either go first or to choose which colour he would like to play. A surprising number of club players elect to forgo the innings in order to choose red or yellow. Several theories are offered for this. The most popular is that the paint of black and blue cause them to swell on hot days. Another is that blue and black are 'harder to see'. Neither seems to bother the top-class players to any marked degree who will always prefer to elect to go first.

The weight of the contemporary croquet ball is sixteen ounces, 'plus or minus a quarter ounce' and there is an interesting regulation concerning its rebounding ability. The balls are tested, by dropping them onto a steel plate one-inch thick, set in rigid concrete. According to the Laws, a ball 'must rebound to a height of not less than thirty inches and not more than forty-five inches'. In addition, the rebound heights of any set of balls used in a game must not be different by more than three inches.

Three types of balls are currently popular: the Jaques Eclipse, Walker balls and the Southport or Birkdale. All three have their devotees and their detractors but the first is the one usually adopted by the Croquet Association for official tournaments.

The clips have always been regarded as 'necessary evils'. They are important, as they announce the state of the game but as any player knows, they are irritatingly easy to forget to take off or replace and no-one has yet discovered the correct method of carrying them during a turn. They can be made of plastic or metal. Metal are the most common at tournaments and each clip is coloured according to the colour of the balls. The player removes the clip as he makes a hoop and their position – on the crown of the hoop when going round the first time and on one of the uprights when coming back, indicates at once what is the state of play. It is up to each player to leave his clips correctly in position – and thereby to monitor his score.

The early game settings usually had two pegs, one for starting and finishing, the other, for turning. They were set out at each end of the court, rather like cricket stumps and painted in the same colours as the balls. The present 'Willis' setting which uses only one centre peg, was adopted in 1922. The peg stands about eighteen inches above the ground and is usually made of wood (though it can be of metal). It carries a thin extension of about six inches, which is used to hold the clips and can be removed if it 'impedes' the striker. This extension was formerly in the shape of a small cross bar and seems to have been somewhat thinner and even less secure than the contemporary regulatory half-inch in diameter.

One of the most important elements of any croquet game is the state of the grass. Precision players love the flat, fast lawns which require a poetic delicacy of touch, an ability to place a ball within a millimetre of its desired position. Others, are as Nora Elvey would say, 'hitters' and can manage better on a 'rougher' surface. All, however, depend on the condition of a good lawn.

In the early days, preparing a lawn seems to have been quite a performance, which may well account for the fact that many of those which feature as the backdrop in early photographs, are an astonishing spread of tufty, coarse grass and rough ground. In their lack of smooth refinement, these lawns seem a direct descendent of the mix of powdered cockle shells on which the game of paille maille, or pell mell, was played.

Lawns were scythed, then rolled before mowing with huge machines which involved a great deal of pushing and pulling and where horsepower was sometimes called upon to ease the burden. According to the Rev. Elvey, some establishments used 'donkeys or ponies shod with leather'. He recommended careful fertilization, attention to wormcasts and deplored the unfortunate practice of playing on wet lawns after morning rain which prevented the lawns from being mown. He felt it not only 'produces conditions trying to the players but must often "break the hearts" of the groundsmen who have been trying so very hard to have the lawns in extra good condition' for forthcoming tournaments.

Good club groundsmen are deservedly legendary. Those who have contributed to the perfection of croquet lawns include Tom Grey, who was head groundsman at Hurlingham for fifty years and Tom Mewett, who cared for the lawns at Compton in East Sussex for some thirty years until forced to retire from eye trouble at the age of eighty-one. The author is fortunate enough to have played at Compton while Tom Mewett was still active and in charge. Nothing can compare with the perfection of his beautifully mown grass and crisp white lines on an early summer morning before a tournament except perhaps, the lawns at Hurlingham. The July 1972 copy of the gazette carried a photograph of Tom Grey on his rolling machine. The size of a steam roller, complete with number plate, three rollers and various cogs and crankshafts – it looked an impressive piece of equipment. Though nothing which the serious-faced Tom, loftily-seated, boot proprietorially astride a connecting girder, could not handle.

In 1920, the Ground Manager of the Bowdon Club rather quaintly laid out the qualifications for a good groundsman and summarized the duties of the job thus:

'A groundsman's work is emphatically an all-the-year-round job, which statement may surprise some people. When snow or hard frost puts a decided stop to work on the lawns, there are always hoops to be painted, seats to varnish, fences to mend, paint or tar, compost heaps to turn – no end in fact to the odd jobs to which a good man may turn his hand and save outside labour. And here perhaps it may be suggested that is it work eminently suited to partly disabled ex-service men. Our own groundsman is totally deaf from shell shock in Gallipoli and had

had no previous experience of the work beyond a few months employment as garden boy before and after the war. All instructions have to be written down for him, but he has well repaid us for the extra trouble in training him, and improved very much physically and mentally from the quiet outdoor life and healthy work.'

The same writer had much to say on the care and maintenance of croquet lawns and placed great store on the weeding, seeding and feeding process. He described how the lawns at Bowdon were originally set down. 'They were laid out and sown by a good firm in 1911, played on in 1912 and used for an Open tournament in 1913 and 1914. During 1916, 1917 and 1918, they were pretty much left to themselves, and suffered accordingly. With great difficulty, they were brought into a fairly playable condition for the 1919 season but the winter work of 1919–20 was long and arduous.' This involved multiple dressing of a variety of substances, including lime, beech compost and hen manure. The latter, it seems was not a great success as large patches of clover appeared but a valuable wartime compost of lawn mowings, vegetable refuse and lime, treated the lawns much better.

Much more recently, *Country Life* magazine carried an article on laying down a croquet lawn. Once again, the emphasis was on seeding, weeding and feeding, and also, given the warm summers of recent years, on frequent watering. This is a subject of some debate amongst croquet players. There is no doubt that watering is essential to protect the grass and to maintain that beautiful greenness which is so envied by visitors from dryer climes, but players who like fast lawns are often reluctant to have them 'slowed' during tournaments by an overnight soaking. In some countries however, watering is not a matter of merely dampening a good 'fast' lawn but of preservation and in a chapter titled 'The Lust for Lawns' in the book *Winning Croquet; from Backyard to Greensward* Jack Osborn and Jesse Kornbluth put installing an irrigation system at the top of their list of priorities.

The Americans play on a variety of turfs and 'smooth' lawns are often a matter of close cutting more than years of top dressing and spiking. Some experimentation has been carried out at home and abroad with artificial lawns. An indoor carpet was tried out in the Sixties and revived in recent years in an attempt to extend the season through the winter. Not everyone is enthusiastic. Those players who have tried the surface generally find the balls 'skid' and are less easy to control and, it seems, even these 'perfect' lawns can have their drawbacks as the neatest carpet can sometimes develop an irritating wrinkle around the hoops which refuses to lie flat. In some of the more recent trials, ball imprints appeared on the surface of the carpet. After much deliberation, it was decided that these were caused by friction between the carpet and the balls. These and other minor imperfections seem to necessitate an excessive amount of brushing and hoovering – probably more hard work in the long run than mowing a real lawn. However useful they are for practice purposes during inclement weather, it is hard to imagine that these artificial surfaces could ever replace the natural greensward. A croquet lawn is justifiably an object of great pride, whether it is the full-sized, much manicured product of a club, or the result of personal planning on a smaller but no less important scale. And as with most art, imperfections often add to the beauty so that 'the dip at third hoop' becomes a much loved feature – as well as a useful item of 'local knowledge' for the home player.

Lawns are probably the biggest divide between the association or club players and those thousands of people who simply enjoy a game of garden croquet. The difference is rather like playing snooker on a full-size table and a game of bar billiards. Both have their elements of enjoyment and in some ways the two are complementary – Once a player has got used to the former however, he is less likely to be 'satisfied' with the latter. Beginners are often encouraged to play on half-size lawns because it 'brings the game in'. The theory is that they are less overawed by the difficulty of placing long shots near far away hoops and, with the game in closer focus, they can concentrate on the tactics. Of course, it's a good idea. Yet it also seems to detract something from the game. However hard it may be to achieve, there is nothing so satisfying to the beginner as to succeed in making an accurate roll or split shot which sends the balls gliding across that vast, green expanse, to, more or less, the desired point. It's only then that he begins to appreciate the full meaning of the term 'equipment' and to enjoy the unbeatable combination of mallet, ball and perfect lawn surface.

THE CHAMPIONS
'Croquet is Just a State of Mind'
John Solomon

[C] roquet has no international seeding system. However, in 1978, Stephen Mulliner produced a national list of computer rankings, based on predicted results which are then adjusted (usually after every game) according to the actual results. Every open game is recorded and a grade calculated for each player. The player loses points for any loss and gains points for a win. A player who has been graded rather low on the list can therefore make enormous progress up the chart during a single season if his performance turns out to be unpredictably good. The system was generally adopted by the Croquet Association in 1988 despite the misgivings of some who felt that in croquet, more than in most games, simply winning does not necessarily make a player 'the best'.

That said, it is no doubt true that most croquet players do like to win, that a fierce spirit of competition haunts the lawns and that everyone who first observes the game wants to know who is the current number one.

According to the computer rankings, Stephen Mulliner is currently Great Britain's national top player. Now in his mid-thirties, he is undoubtedly at the very peak of his game. A rather intense man, noted for his speed about the lawns and his habit of 'posturing' before the hoops to line up his shots with surgical precision (often lying flat on his stomach to peer into the 'jaws'), his earlier failures seemed almost always to have been caused by nerves. But success bred confidence –

and more success. In 1988, he defeated Nigel Aspinall to win the Open Championship, having suffered the position of bridesmaid on several previous occasions. His victory gave him the burst of confidence he needed and marked a turning point in his croquet career. Since then he has been unstoppable, not only on the lawns at home and abroad (he played a fine series of games in New Zealand during the 1990 Test match) but in the administration of the game. An investment banker, Mulliner has a fine appreciation of finance which is somewhat rare in croquet administration. He has put his energy, when off the lawns, into encouraging sponsorship in the game and into his work as chairman of the Finance and General Purposes Committee for the four years to 1988. As former vice-chairman of the CA, he recently took over as Chairman. Meanwhile he has been busy producing a series of books on the game.

The best of these to date, *The World of Croquet*, co-authored with the chairman of the Croquet Association's coaching committee, John McCullough, was published in 1987. It is an excellent introduction for anyone interested in taking up the association game. Perhaps the most interesting chapter however, is that entitled 'Inner Croquet'.

Sports Psychology is not a term one readily associates with croquet. The popular image of the game, which cherishes a vision of warm afternoons serenaded by the gentle clunk of balls while one player slowly makes his way across the lawns and his partner snoozes in a chair on the sidelines, does not equate easily with the concept of 'pressure'. But in the present game of association croquet, pressure is all too common. Every player knows the frustration of having hit a ball badly, stuck in a hoop or broken down in some other fashion during a carefully constructed break. It is hard enough when performed 'privately' and doubtless even harder when under the critical eye of spectators.

'Temperament' is a subject which is accorded a great deal of importance amongst croquet players in New Zealand and Australia where the ability to maintain concentration, to be totally unaffected by failure and to demonstrate great patience is regarded as a vital component in the make-up of any croquet player. Anyone with an 'attitude problem' is automatically suspect.

The British players, like the Americans, generally appear to allow more room for an attitude, if only as an expression of individuality.

However, Mulliner and McCullough took a very serious look at the matter. They advised the player to separate the subconscious from the conscious and allow the former to take control. Practice is the first priority in discovering potential and lulling the conscious mind into quiescence is the key to improving performance. It is a fascinating chapter and Stephen Mulliner obviously practises and has profited from, all he preaches.

During the 1990 Test match, Keith Aiton as coach, noted that once Mulliner was able to forget the awesome reputation of some of his opponents and treat his game as if it were 'an ordinary championships at home', he could overcome any tendency to match nerves.

Knowing he *can* win has obviously made a difference to Mulliner's game but in addition he has always *wanted* to win. The will to win is a curious factor in any game psychology. The player needs the drive of incentive but too much determination and the desire is often frustrated. This plays a particular role in croquet. In many other games, a player generally falls from physical peak. He finds that he just isn't fast enough or fit anymore. In croquet, because in theory, anyone can play at any age, the physical factor applies less rigorously. Players can take up the game in middle age and still reach top form or make extraordinary 'comebacks' which do not simply last for one magical season, but continue over several years. At other times, the 'conscious' mind takes over, doubt creeps in, the desire to win becomes overwhelming and defeat is increasingly difficult to take philosophically. In the end, more players in croquet are defeated by 'psychology' than by any other factor.

One of the greatest players of the last fifty years took the time and trouble to try to explain this sudden wave of 'over-analysis' which seems to swamp every top-class player at some stage in his career. John Solomon dominated British croquet for nearly thirty years. He won forty-eight national titles, including that of Champion of Champions on the only four occasions on which it was played, represented Great Britain in five Test tours and won the New Zealand singles twice. His fame as a croquet player was (and remains) truly international.

Solomon made his first official appearance in croquet as a schoolboy. He had learnt to play at home, encouraged by his mother who had taken up croquet at the Roehampton Club. Later, his father also developed a keen interest in the game, so much so that he forsook his own sport of bowls.

Solomon was still a pupil at Charterhouse when he won his first competition at Roehampton at the end of 1947. The following year, he entered for the Longworth Cup at Hurlingham. Ironically, his opponent was one of the 'old school', Miss Lydia Elphinstone Stone who had made her own debut at Maidstone in 1895.

The same year, he won the Men's handicap Doubles and his handicap, which had started at ten, fell to two. On the way back to school, he spent his time on the train working out how to do a triple peel. It was characteristic that he should have puzzled it out for himself and in the process, turned up with something more interesting than the standard tactic (in this case it was the straight triple). It was an illustration of the 'enterprise' he was to bring to many aspects of the game.

Solomon soon startled the croquet world. He was not only the youngest player who had come to the game since the war and supremely talented, but he brought to croquet a dash and style that was quite unique. He seemed to be able to play any shot with ease and the overall impression was one of relaxed, rhythmical movement. Everything appeared to go right for him and he seemed prepared to take risks and get away with it. He combined a sharply enquiring mind with the instinct of the gambler and was never averse to trying something new in tactics, or for that matter, in debunking some of the former 'myths' of good play. He had, for example, a deep dislike of the old front style which he felt was utterly wrong. He was equally averse to consultations between partners in Open Doubles, describing the practice as an 'appalling aspect' of the game.

His opinion on technique and tactical matters was set forth with great authority in his book, *Croquet*, (first published in 1966) probably the most readable book of advanced croquet tactics ever written. The tone of the book and his performance on the lawns make it hard to imagine him ever suffering from match nerves. Yet suffer he did. In some ways he found these initial 'butterflies' helped his game and when, with increasing success, they began to disappear, he almost missed them. In 1950, he left with the British team for his first Test tour in New Zealand. He was the baby of the group, with such veterans as Humphrey Hicks leading the way and though Great Britain lost by the series, Solomon won a singles match against Clem Watkins, another against Ashley Heenan and all three doubles in which he played with Humphrey Hicks and Ward Petley who had travelled up from South

Africa. This trip with all its wonderful sights and sounds (and teas and suppers) must have been a marvellous 'initiation' for a young player (as no doubt it was to be for Mark Saurin in 1990) and on his return to England in 1951, Solomon probably already considered himself something of an 'old hand' at the game. He was nineteen, in between school and Cambridge where he planned to read music – the other great love of his life – and with nothing to do but play croquet for a year. He seems to have made good use of it. He defeated Geoffrey Reckitt to win a Gold Medal, had a fierce battle against Humphrey Hicks in the Open Championships, played at Cheltenham and Southwick (where he had another extraordinary game, this time against Willy Longman, which Solomon won) and was lauded in a poem by Maurice Reckitt.

By this time, his shooting ability had become legendary. Over the next few years, he concentrated on the major tournaments (mainly for lack of time). In 1953, he won his first Open Championship against Humphrey Hicks and was elected to the Croquet Association Council and two years later, he won the President's Cup, reserved for the best players. For the next decade, Solomon triumphed. The only person who seemed able to stop him was the formidable Humphrey Hicks and like the great H. O., he had one year in which he won every event he entered. (For Solomon this was 1959. H. O. Hicks' year of superlative triumph was 1948 when he played the six leading tournaments of the year and did not lose a match in singles.)

The praise was fulsome. Maurice Reckitt called Solomon a 'magician' and indeed, there seems to have been something magical about the grace and ease with which this slight, slim figure weaved his way about the courts.

In 1969, he captained the British team in Australia. In the first Test, he met up with another legend, John Prince, but Solomon was unwell and, although Britain won the series, it was a disastrous start to a personally unsatisfactory tour. He was beginning to suffer from the strain of having a 'reputation' to maintain. Like an author on his second 'bestseller' who begins to polish every phrase and finds that he cannot write a single satisfactory line, Solomon found himself getting pernickity about the position of balls on the court, something which had never troubled him in the past. It signalled a subtle change in his hitherto 'carefree approach' to the game. New players were up and coming and they began to rattle him slightly. The game which had come so naturally to him, seemed suddenly to require more thought. And the more he thought about it, the harder it became to play. Knowing how well he had played in the past, he felt frustrated and furious that he was no longer able to command the same easy success. By 1978, the doubt had become aggravated by desire. Players were battling for selection for the next Test and Solomon desperately wanted to be included, not just to preserve his record but to renew many of the friendships he had made earlier. Some observers, watching him fall from form, thought he was suffering from 'hoopitis'. Solomon himself concluded that his nerves came on with all single-ball shots.

He worried about his style, thinking that it must have altered in some subtle way. His wrist control appeared to have gone so that the 'surgeon's grip, firm but flexible' was lost. Instead, his wrists seemed to twist out of his control and the only way he could stop that small flick was to grip his mallet 'like a vice'. This new grip was uncomfortable to one who had always played with such a loose, easy movement but all the time it seemed to work, he persevered.

He also experimented with his swing and the distance from which he played a shot. He even tried getting 'stoned' in an effort to calm his nerves but though this worked initially he soon found that, drunk or sober, the nerves returned. It was no way to go on and sensibly, he decided to stop.

Solomon had already tried a sabbatical. He had taken two years away from the game between 1976 and 1978 but when he returned all the old pressure was there. Perhaps the fact that he, as well as everyone else, expected him to qualify for the forthcoming Test, made it inevitable that he would simply try too hard. His reputation for success stood before him like a brick wall and his friends were as uncomfortable as he was. Prichard wrote that it was 'sad to see him struggling to regain his form without success'.

In some ways one cannot help but wonder if Solomon was not also a victim of changing attitudes to the game. The 'cerebral approach' was beginning to take hold, an attitude which he had never approved of and which was completely contrary to his own intuitive brilliance. He rarely takes up a mallet these days, being more interested in golf, but when he does, the old magic is still there. It is a great pity that his skill has not been used more in coaching or in exhibition games which could introduce more people to croquet. He is a witty and relaxed commentator and has an ability to make a complicated game comprehensible to the beginner without losing any of the reference to the advanced technique and tactics which make croquet so interesting. As President of the Croquet Association, he still keeps a keen eye on croquet affairs and can be seen about the lawns occasionally with his wife who also plays, watching a major tournament and perhaps feeling gratified that, young as today's rising stars are, he was younger than any of them when he first took croquet by storm.

Long before John Solomon reached his crisis of confidence, the then Vice-Chairman of Council, Dr Wiggins gave the following useful advice to tournament players: 'Contrary to general belief, tobacco does not steady the nerves and its smoke does not improve vision. Reading should be reduced during a competition week and only the larger headlines of the newspapers read. This rests the visual focusing apparatus. Never think, "I must hit this one". You won't. Result – Nervous tension. Avoidance of heavy manual work for forty-eight hours before and during the competition. Medicinally, a preprandial small quantity of alcohol is helpful. Larger quantities – fatal.'

Solomon's decision to quit play rather than to simply fade from the scene, was shared by another of his great contemporaries. At one time, Hicks and Solomon were part of a triumvirate. The third was E. P. C. Cotter.

Unlike John Solomon, Pat Cotter achieved croquet greatness comparatively late in life. He was in his forties when he won the Gilbey Cup at Roehampton in 1947 but like most players, he had also played as a child. He was given a croquet set when he was seven and remembers playing at his home in Bedford in a series of hot summers. It was in Ireland however, where his father was stationed in the Army that he began to play seriously. He was then sixteen and played with a handicap of four before drifting away from the game until many years later.

He started his 1947 season with a handicap of nine and ended it at one and a half. From then on he surged ahead, winning the President's Cup six times, the Open Championship three times and the Open Doubles Championship in which he played with John Solomon, a remarkable ten times. He also captained the English team against New Zealand in their triumphant Test in 1963 but his happiest memory is beating the veteran Monty Spencer-Ell at Roehampton in a game where Cotter came from a trailing position at second hoop to win by three points.

Like John Solomon, Cotter bestrode two croquet eras. He played against D. D. Steel at Devonshire Park in Eastbourne, defeating her with a combination peg out and played most of his mixed doubles with

Daisy Lintern. He defeated John Solomon four times for the President's cup (three of them after tie) and feels that he was only denied winning a seventh time because his Abyssinian cat got caught in a tree and Cotter spent the night advising the fire brigade on how best to retrieve the creature.

As a classics master at St Paul's school, Cotter had little time to take any croquet sabbaticals. He received generous time off for Test matches and concentrated his efforts on the major events but having decided to bring his formidable attention to bear on croquet, he determined to master the game in every way. One great contribution was in reviving the triple peel which had temporarily fallen from favour with the introduction, in 1946 of the second lift. 'When I came into the game, people just didn't do triple peels. H. O. Hicks was a very sound player, accurate and difficult to beat, but he never went in for triple peeling,' recalls Cotter. He and John Solomon revised and revived the triple and in the process, they can claim to have bettered the standard of the game.

They were complementary opposites. John Solomon had the quick intuitive mind that was happy to take risks in the pursuit of novelty. Cotter's approach was more cautious and more profoundly analytical but together, they turned croquet into a game of intellectual skill. In the introduction to his book on the subject (*Tackle Croquet This Way*, Stanley Paul and Co., 1960), Cotter wrote that 'many games have suffered through the years from an unintelligent lack of appreciation'. He and Solomon instilled in croquet the appreciation which at association level, it continues to enjoy today. They showed that it is not only a good game and a skilful one but a game full of variety and possibility for the player prepared to explore its depths. And in the process, Cotter, like Solomon, gradually became a little disillusioned. 'I feel that the absolute fighting edge goes off when you've won so much,' he now reflects. Like Solomon, he found the expectation that he should continue to win increasingly cumbersome but he was also drawn away from the game by other interests. An international bridge player, he has long been the bridge correspondent of both the *Financial Times* and *Country Life* and also enjoys a reputation as a first-class compiler of crosswords. At one time, he contributed articles on tactics to the gazette and even wrote about bridge but when he finally gave up playing, his disappearance from the croquet scene was complete. He too might have taken up coaching or exhibition play.

Instead, he switched his attention away from croquet with as much force as he had originally focused on it, though in private, he still speaks of the game with enthusiasm.

Cotter and Solomon represent a revival in the intellectual approach to croquet which contributed far more to the modern game than mere entries in the record books. The gap they left by their departure from the game was soon taken up by a new wave of contemporary heroes, chief among them Keith Wylie and Nigel Aspinall.

Since he got married a few years ago, Keith Wylie has more or less deserted croquet. He still corresponds with the gazette and occasionally can be seen on the lawns, looking long-legged as a stork. Mention of his name brings a smile to the faces of all who know him. His wit and self-confidence, his ability to 'always use three words instead of one', his panache and tactical brilliance on the croquet court are all mourned in passing. He appeared on the scene at about the same time as Nigel Aspinall and was soon described as a 'perfectionist'. In 1970 and 1971, he defeated Aspinall to take the Open Championship, the only two times he won it. He also won the President's Cup twice, once in 1967 and in 1977, when he again defeated Aspinall.

The latter now forms the last link between the Cotter and Solomon era of the Sixties and the present one. When Aspinall started playing, the original 'circuit' – the social round of tournaments described in chapter five – was still very much in existence. Indeed, his very first defeat in tournament play (in 1965) was at the hands of one of the old circuit regulars, Commander Giles Borrett.

Nigel Aspinall was in some ways John Solomon's designated heir. He shared the same natural style, delicate touch and enterprise which seemed to Solomon to 'be exactly the right combination'. It was against Aspinall that Solomon played his final championship and he was led to conclude that the young man 'is the greatest player of our time and quite possibly the greatest of all time'. (Though he also said the same about Humphrey Hicks on another occasion.)

This was in 1979. Aspinall had won his first tournament in 1965 and since then, had slowly played his way to the top, though one or two of the 'old stagers' were determined not to make his path an easy one. He played Humphrey Hicks in the Opens in 1966 winning the first game easily enough but being outmanoeuvred by the old master in the last two games. But already, the commentators were euphoric in their praise of Aspinall. They called him 'the Happy Warrior', and the 'complete croquet player' and described him as 'lean, swift and with a long shot unbettered in a period of brilliant marksmanship'. They also predicted that he would go far in the forthcoming Test match in Australia where he was bound to 'delight all who watch and meet him'.

They were right. 1969 was Aspinall's year. He won the Open Championship in a sensational match against John Solomon. One commentator wrote in the gazette that, 'It was one of those games in which the spectator's sympathies veered desperately from one side to another, but it was impossible to grudge the success to the dashing young challenger, one of the most attractive performers of this decade.' Aspinall also won all his matches in the Test series, including that against the New Zealand champion John Prince, which for many, left him as the unofficial world champion. After that, it was merely a case of collecting more titles (and trophies) and by the mid-Eighties, Aspinall was only a half dozen or so away from John Solomon's record.

A Physics and General Science graduate from Bristol University, Aspinall had a brief career as a computer programmer but as croquet slowly took over his life, he gave up work. Had he been a professional coach or player, he would have made a lot of money from the game. As it was, he seemed content to divide his time, unrewarded except by satisfaction, between the lawns and the CA Council of which he became a member in 1970.

In recent years he has found it harder to close the gap between his own and Solomon's record. He was defeated by Stephen Mulliner for the President's Cup in 1986 and for the Open Championship in 1988. In 1989, he was put out of the World Singles Championship by a complete newcomer, Steve Comish.

It is unlikely that Aspinall suffers from the same 'pressure to win' that afflicted Solomon and, to a lesser degree, Cotter. A very self-contained and somewhat solitary man, Aspinall has always been largely unmoved by spectator opinion or the need to do well to please others. He has said he hopes to go on playing croquet for as long as he enjoys it and though he obviously enjoys it at present, he seems becalmed. His reputation among croquet players remains high and his contribution is by no means over although he seems to be waiting for a fair wind to set him back on course. Perhaps the prospect of taking those last few titles will be enough. It would certainly be a sadness if a player of his style and great experience were simply to slip away.

One of Mulliner and Aspinall's closest contemporary rivals is Mark

117

Avery. Still in his early twenties, Avery is another who first played croquet as a child. On top form, his play is nothing short of sensational but his performance can be erratic. He was comprehensively beaten by Aspinall in the quarter finals of the Men's Championship in 1983 and had such an unsuccessful season in 1986 that it was rumoured he was about to give up the game. Fortunately, he returned the following year when he played a gripping final in the Open Championship to defeat Stephen Mulliner. In 1988, he temporarily left England to take up the offer of a post as a professional coach in the United States. The move caused some excitement at the time, not least in the national press. Avery was being lured by 'big money'. He was to become the first 'croquet professional'. In fact, the whole project fell through and he returned to the home courts in time to win the Western Championships in the spring of 1989.

Avery would no doubt agree with Nigel Aspinall that 'if you're good at something it seems entirely reasonable to want to make a living out of it'. His 'defection' raised a few eyebrows at home but they soon settled again when he wasted no time in re-establishing himself on the courts. In 1989 he gave his finest performance to date in the World Championships. He played a series of quality matches, including one against New Zealand champion Bob Jackson, which brought him into the finals against Joe Hogan, New Zealand's number one. And what a final it was. Some 200 people gathered round the lawn at Hurlingham to watch – a capacity crowd for croquet. Avery could have been expected to feel great pressure, playing as he was before his peers but he appeared completely relaxed. No attitude problem here. He reached four-back and was well launched on a triple peel when he stuck in a hoop. Hogan went on to win this game and then the second, but throughout, Avery's play had been a delight to watch. The scores of both games – plus three (the maximum score is +26) – are evidence of how close the competition was.

Much later, Avery remarked that he thought his approach had been a little too casual. 'I was a bit too confident, especially playing someone like Hogan and I made two vital errors at crucial times in the match.'

However, Avery is not a man to let defeat weigh on him too heavily. He was selected for the 1990 Test when Britain regained the MacRobertson Shield from the holders, New Zealand. Once again he lost to Joe Hogan (this time by a larger margin) but found his form sufficiently with David Openshaw as partner, to beat Hogan and Jackson in the doubles.

David Openshaw is one of croquet's stalwarts. Now in his early forties, he has captained the British Test team three times. No doubt his dry sense of humour and his steadiness have done much to help establish the camaraderie necessary to hold a good team together. He has earned a reputation as a careful tactician and also for scraping home through a tight finish. One of his finest matches was in the quarter finals of the World Championship in 1989 when he gave a perfect demonstration of the art of the gritty fighter (see p.138).

In their time, all the above players have stood above the crowd which is no mean achievement, especially as today, the crowd itself is packed with good players. There are the 'Cambridge set' who all played at university which includes Richard Hilditch, Keith Aiton, a master of precision and Dayal Gunasekera, a player of such flowing style that he is a delight to watch. Hilditch overlaps into the 'Welsh set', which has at some time included all three Prichard siblings and which in turn, includes one of contemporary croquet's two Williams; William Prichard and William Ormerod. The latter had a terrific struggle against Nigel Aspinall in the 1973 President's Cup (though Aspinall won the cup with overall number of wins). Writing about him a year later, a commentator in the gazette said, 'Ormerod follows his ball about the courts after huge but accurate split shots, with slow measured tread, resolute but serene; one is aware of a formidable croquet intelligence at work.'

William Prichard played in the 1990 Test and proved that he still has 'beautiful touch'. His family are croquet fanatics and have been known to overwhelm the lawns by sheer force of numbers. A spectator writing about the end of season tournament at Devonshire Park in the mid-Seventies was moved to comment on this 'Permutation of Prichards' who on that occasion, walked off with six first, and four second, prizes.

Then there are the 'newcomers', who, like Solomon made their first appearances while still at school and have astonished everyone with their talent. Chief among these are Chris Clarke, Robert Fulford and Mark Saurin.

Chris Clarke shot to fame in 1988 when he won the National Junior Championship in July and then swept a field of 'old stagers' to take the President's Cup. At this time he was still a schoolboy from Blackburn, a pupil of Andrew Bennet, a French teacher whose enthusiasm and dedication to croquet has introduced several young people to the association game.

Within the space of three years Chris Clarke had reached three consecutive championship titles. His performance had been quite remarkable and he was bitterly disappointed therefore, when he failed to be selected for the 1990 Test, especially as his doubles partner, Robert Fulford, was chosen. Fulford is one of croquet's natural gentlemen and an excellent player. Quiet, rather shy, he has won his way to the top with consistency and concentration. He won the President's Cup in 1989 and accompanied by Chris Clarke, fought his way to the finals of the Doubles in the World Championship. He and his opponent were despatched by those two veterans of New Zealand croquet, Joe Hogan and Bob Jackson, but they had already beaten a strong field. By the end of 1989 Fulford already looked set for a long and successful croquet career and in 1990 he crowned his achievements by winning the World Championships.

Mark Saurin is also a product of Andrew Bennet's teaching. Mark had played croquet for several years at school with his two younger brothers. A pleasant, approachable young man, he was the youngest member of the 1990 Test team (and was subsequently dubbed 'the nipper'). The experience confirmed his love of croquet and his determination to play and travel more. His more than usually 'open' reaction to bad shots, his 'exuberant and adventurous play' may be part of youthful enthusiasm but he has a thoughtfulness that is beyond his years and a determination that should take him far.

Champions come and go in croquet as in every other sport. Some go more quickly than others but a few go down in history. When Steve Davis first won his way to snooker fame, he was greeted with the usual surprise and delight that is accorded to all winners in life. Gradually however, he passed from being a 'novelty' to proving himself one of the greatest ever technicians of snooker and his game slowly matured to vintage point. The same is true of John Solomon. His day may have passed but his presence has left an indelible mark. Not only does his record still stand unbeaten but few have come near to matching the maverick skill he brought to croquet.

In croquet as in many sports, each age has its heroes and in answer to every new talent there will always be those who say, 'Ah but you should have seen so and so . . . ' Individual games can count as much as long records: Openshaw's second game against Mulliner in the World

Championships, Avery's match against Hogan or even Phil Cordingly's game against Aspinall in the President's Cup in 1983 when, after a protracted struggle which over-ran into the next day, he 'hit fair and square to record a splendid win'. It may even be true that in croquet the people who really matter are not those who win at all but simply those who play. It is, after all, 'a state of mind'.

THE GAME OF CROQUET
Tactics and How to Win

*The chief difficulty Alice found at first was in managing her
flamingo. She succeeded in getting its body tucked away, comfortably enough, under her arm, with its legs hanging down, but generally, just as she had got its neck nicely straightened out and was
going to give the hedgehog a blow with its head, it would twist itself
round and look up in her face, with such a puzzled expression that
she could not help bursting out laughing; and, when she had got its
head down, and was going to begin again, it was very provoking to
find that the hedgehog had unrolled itself, and was in the act of
crawling away; besides all this, there was generally a ridge or a
furrow in the way wherever she wanted to send the hedgehog to,
and, as the doubled-up soldiers were always getting up and walking
off to other parts of the ground, Alice soon came to the conclusion
that it was a very difficult game indeed.*

L ewis Carroll has been much condemned for his part in making
croquet sound the most silly of sports. His description of Alice's
confrontation with the Queen's croquet ground is said to have
convinced generations that croquet is a pointless pastime.

Be that as it may, the passage quoted above shows a remarkably
perceptive view of the psychology of the game. For there is no doubt
that croquet is difficult and that at any level, it really can be a most
'provoking' game.

This is largely due to the unpredictable element which can creep in when all is flowing supremely smoothly, to ruin a good break or leave a ball 'stuck in the jaws' of a hoop. Time and again, the 'flamingo factor' raises its head and not all players have the good nature of Alice and can console themselves so readily with a burst of laughter.

Most of us who have played 'garden croquet' have experience of this. We tend to blame our inadequacies on the court, which at private houses, exhibits an astonishing variation of size and condition. There are those for whom a tree represents a centre peg, or who delight in the local knowledge that there is a 'dip in the lawn' at third hoop. The boundary is rarely marked, as courts are often temporary, and for this reason too, the grass may also be rather long. Most distracting of all will be the variation in rules. Nowadays, most croquet manufacturers include a copy of the Laws of the Croquet Association, the body which governs the game, with each new set of hoops and mallets. Even so, some of the bitterest croquet confrontations take place at informal croquet gatherings over the vexed question of just what you are 'allowed' to do. On the subject of rules, it so often appears to be the case that 'every one seems to make his own to suit the occasion'.

For this reason, garden croquet can be very unsatisfactory. Just like Alice, the player who thinks he knows how to play, may find himself subjected to a completely different and somewhat arbitrary set of conditions which may prove frustrating in the extreme. The only way to overcome this and ensure that everyone knows what is expected of him is to play by the Laws of the Croquet Association. For the keen player, this has the additional advantage of preparing him for club competitions which are the main route to participation in the major tournaments annually gracing the croquet calendar. Never let the faint-hearted think that this is beyond him. Croquet is a great game, not least because it allows very rapid progress to anyone, male or female, young or older, who is prepared to learn and practise. Association croquet has a handicap system that grades players from eighteen down to minus two (though club handicaps are often higher) and it is not unusual for a good player to reduce his handicap by half during one season.

Those who hanker after the relaxed image of the gentle clunk of mallet against ball played to a background symphony of laughing voices and the soft tinkle of ice in tall glasses, need not fear the more 'professional' world of association croquet. Major tournaments take place in clubs around the country where willing helpers tend the bar, produce the tea and maintain the atmosphere of civilized sport that characterizes croquet. During the first World Championships held at Hurlingham in the long hot summer of 1989, a string quartet played in the background as a small crowd of spectators sprawled in deck chairs beneath the shady trees to watch the new world champion bring his game quietly to a close. No cheering masses, no wild demonstrations of gleeful emotion from the victor, no television. Somebody gave a short speech and, during the presentation, somebody else dropped and dented the heavy antique silver cup. Perhaps he tripped on a hedgehog.

Croquet, therefore, continues to maintain a degree of unpredictable eccentricity at all levels but despite this relaxed approach, association croquet is a highly organized game. To play it, or simply to get enjoyment from watching a top level game, one needs to know what is going on. There is a debate in croquet circles that it is not and never will be a 'spectator sport', which accounts for its hitherto low media profile. The argument in favour of this view is that much of top level play is so tactical that it becomes boring to the mere on-looker. This may be true for some, including those of us who think we already 'know' the game but surely, all that is needed to improve this situation is to give the spectator a basic understanding of how association croquet is played.

With that in mind, here is a basic introduction to the game of croquet which may help the complete newcomer and even the keen garden player to understand the great possibilities of playing at a more advanced level and may also give the casual spectator a degree of knowledge with which he can begin to enjoy the game.

How Croquet is Played

The object of the game of croquet is to drive two balls, in the correct order, through six hoops, first one way then back the other way, scoring twelve points for each ball. The balls are then 'pegged out' scoring another two points, making a total of twenty-six. The winner is the first to score the total and the difference between this and the number of points achieved by the loser is the final score of the game. Thus, if the winner makes all the hoops and his opponent makes none, he wins by the maximum score +26. If the opponent has scored, say ten points, he has lost −16 (and the winner takes that game +16). In tournaments, players usually compete for the best of three games, thus a score could read something like the following: +26, −26, +26. (This was the winning score for the World Championship Doubles in 1989 in which Hogan and Jackson of New Zealand beat Clarke and Fulford of Great Britain.)

The game is played with four balls coloured blue, red, black and yellow (these colours are repeated on the centre peg) and in singles, blue and black are always played together by one side and, likewise, red and yellow by the other. In doubles, each person plays one ball throughout the game but the 'teams' still play red and yellow against black and blue.

The balls are hit through square metal hoops which are painted white. The top, or 'crown' of the first hoop is coloured blue and the last hoop, which is also known as 'rover' has a red crown. The hoops must be firmly fixed in the ground, with the sides, or 'uprights', parallel and the distance between them not less than three and three-quarter inches and not more than four inches. However, in tournament play the hoops are sometimes 'narrowed' (See the Laws of Association Croquet No 50d).

The centre peg is made of wood and painted with the colours of the balls. It should also be fixed firmly in position. The balls should be three and five eighths of an inch in diameter and weigh about a pound. Most modern balls are made of a composite (see p. 103) and are quite strong as is demonstrated by Law 2c which advises that when dropped from a height of sixty inches onto a one-inch steel plate set in concrete, a croquet ball should not rebound more than forty-five inches or less than thirty inches!

Balls are hit with a mallet, usually made of wood, weighing in total about three and a quarter pounds and a set of four clips, one for each ball and coloured to match, enables the players to monitor the state of the game. The clip matching the ball in play is placed on the hoop (or peg) next in order for that ball. When playing the first six hoops the clips are placed on the crown and when playing the last (back) six, they are clipped to the upright of the hoop. The 'court' is a flat rectangular grass lawn which is thirty-five yards long by twenty-eight yards wide. The boundaries are marked with a white line.

Before beginning play, one side tosses a coin. The winner can take the choice of lead – in other words to play first, or he can choose the colours. If he elects to play first, his opponent has choice of colours and vice versa. Many people have a preference for the yellow and red balls, and there is some debate as to whether black and blue are 'harder to see' or that the paint of the black ball causes it to run less smoothly and 'drag' across the lawn. Most experienced players, however, choose to play first and will carefully hit the ball to place it on the boundary near the fourth hoop. This is in contradiction to the normal practice of garden croquet which is simply to aim straight for the first hoop. The move is one which straight away separates the 'amateurs' from the 'professionals'. For the art of association croquet lies in using all the balls to set up 'breaks', as in a game of snooker.

For this reason, the good player considers that making one hoop means little. He hopes to get all the balls in position so that he can play each of them in turn to make a series of hoops. His intention at the start of the game therefore, is to keep away from the first hoop where he could give his partner an easy shot and to wait until all the balls are in play. Once this happens, he tries to set up a break.

As in snooker, each player takes turns alternately and has one shot on which he tries to build additional 'continuation' shots. With skill and luck, a croquet player can go on to end the game before his partner has even made a hoop. He does this by a series of shots called roquets, croquets and hoop shots.

The first shot in the sequence is the roquet. A player makes a roquet by hitting any one of the other three balls in play with his own ball. This first 'shot' is crucial as it gets him into the game. Should he succeed in 'hitting in' he can then go on to 'take croquet' and set about establishing himself as the 'in player'. If he fails to make a hit, his turn ends (and he becomes the 'out player').

This explains why so many top players concentrate on practising their 'shooting'. Some practise by trying to hit the peg from the boundary lines, others by shooting from the side to the rover hoop. Success lies not only in having a good eye for the direction of the ball and 'stalking' it by approaching the ball slowly from a few paces along the line of aim to check that your body is facing the target. But also, for example, in standing correctly, knowing how to place the feet and hold the mallet, hit the ball square and clean and not lifting the head as the ball takes off.

If he succeeds in hitting, the player then goes on to 'take croquet'. He does this by picking up his own ball (or pushing it with his foot, knocking it along with his mallet) and placing it beside the ball he has roqueted wherever it might have stopped after being hit.

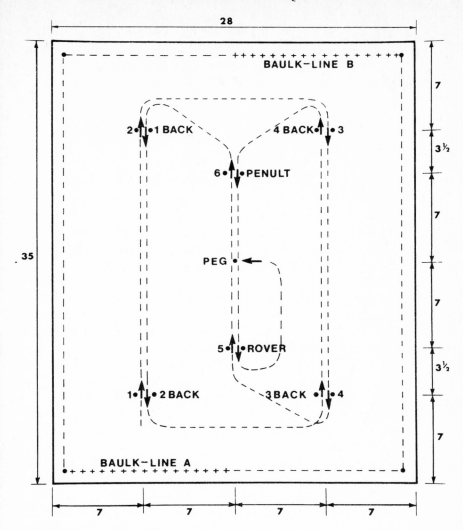

All distances are in yards.

Only the outer continuous line (the Boundary line) is marked on the court.

The Yard-line is one yard from the Boundary line and parallel to it. It is indicated on the plan as a dotted line on which the two starting, or Baulk, lines are shown.

The order of making the hoops is indicated by arrows starting from Hoop No. 1.

The starting hoop has a blue crown and the final, or Rover, hoop has a red crown.

(By courtesy of the Croquet Association.)

127

A few misconceptions can be instantly dealt with here. You may position, nudge, firm down your own ball but you must not move the other – *nor may you put your foot on it* when playing the stroke! Law 32 states quite clearly that a fault is committed during play if a player touches a ball 'with any part of his body or his clothes'. When striking your own ball, the other one need not move any distance but it should at least shake. If it does not move at all, a fault is committed.

The variations on the croquet stroke are numerous and the way each is played dictates what the stroke is called. The main selection are the following:

The Straight Drive consists of placing the two balls one behind the other (your ball, the one you will hit, being nearest to you) and aiming the mallet along the central line of the adjoining balls. In this stroke, the forward ball will obviously travel further than the ball you strike – about three times the distance. In order to make your own ball travel further as well, you need to change your grip and stance to perform a Roll Shot. This consists of moving one hand further down the mallet and standing further forward over the balls in order to get more leverage on the mallet. The further down the shaft you hold the mallet, the more rigid it becomes and the greater the roll (though you must not let your hand touch the head of the mallet) until you can actually make the back ball travel further than the front ball in what is called a 'pass roll'.

The opposite of this kind of shot is called the 'Stop' shot. Here, the back ball is delayed while the front ball travels much further. This is achieved by standing back and hitting the balls with a firm stroke but allowing the mallet to be checked by loosening your grip at the top of the shaft. The looser the grip on the mallet, the less the pressure exerted in the swing and the shorter the distance your own ball will travel.

Straight drives, roll and stop shots are all played with the balls in a line but split shots and take-offs are used to 'angle' shots. Working out angles, like all play in croquet, comes best with practice but a point to remember is that the croqueted ball will always travel along the line joining the centre of the two balls. It is therefore essential to take the utmost care in lining up the balls and working out the direction in which the stroke is aimed. Take-off shots are split shots played at such a wide angle that the croqueted ball (the one that is not hit) hardly travels at all.

There are many ways of playing these shots and they are often described in books of tactics with a wealth of accompanying illustration. This can certainly help the player answer some questions of where and why he is going wrong but, as with any sport, the real path to progress lies in participation and the best way to learn how to make better croquet shots is to join a club and take lessons. The Croquet Association runs special coaching courses each year and one of these can soon turn a garden player into a very competent association player.

Already, we have come a long way from the simple game that involves consistently bashing the opponent into the bushes while slowly plodding ahead through the hoops. This may result in its own degree of success but the player who is competent enough to run hoops consistently can probably get to competition level if he takes a little time to study the real game of croquet.

However, nothing worth doing is really easy and as with Alice's game, things are often slightly more complicated than at first they seem. For example, many of the basic strokes and terms of croquet break down into a series of variations which need to be examined a little more closely. Of these, the following are among the most essential:

'The rush' is one of the most important strokes in the game. It is a form of roquet which the player 'controls'. In other words, he uses the ball he is hitting to propel the roqueted ball to a particular position on the court.

Most players use short rushes to push balls nearer to the hoops so that they can then neatly croquet the balls into position in order to make the hoop tidily. Anything longer than about three yards is no longer a rush but a roquet.

There are two basic kinds of rushes – the 'straight', which is self-explanatory and the 'cut rush', where the ball is hit off-centre and which, as in snooker, requires a greater element of force, depending on the degree of the cut. Neither shot is particularly easy, though good players make it seem so. Some sort of inhibition appears to creep into any attempt by the relatively inexperienced player to 'rush' a ball.

The solution would seem to lie in taking very careful aim, minimizing body movement, maintaining a good, steady swing and not forcing the stroke – all easier said than done, as Alice would no doubt have agreed.

In keeping with the spirit of things being not quite what they seem, the most common stroke in croquet and the one which everyone recognizes instantly, is also one of the hardest.

'Hoop strokes' are vital. If you cannot make the hoop, you cannot score points. So much is obvious but at garden level, a great deal of controversy revolves around the hoop. What happens if you run the hoop from the wrong side? If you push a partner's ball through does he score a point? Can you claim a point if the ball is only half-way through the hoop? The answers are the following: running the hoop from the wrong side results in no score; putting your partner's ball through the hoop gives him a point and if a ball is not completely through a hoop, no point can be scored.

In determining the last of these, it is necessary to remember that the hoop has two sides: the playing side – the side from which the ball approaches and the non-playing side. A ball must have passed the playing side to have run the hoop. In other words, if you can slide the head of the mallet down the uprights of the hoop on the playing side without touching the ball, the hoop has been made.

There are two main types of shot for hoop approaches. They are the 'soft' shot and the 'hard'. In the latter, the player relies on the speed of the ball to propel it through the hoop and gives it a sharp whack. Unfortunately the process often involves a loss of accuracy. Many a top-class player has been seen to play his ball hard into a hoop, leaving it frustratingly 'stuck in the jaws'.

More reliable is the soft shot where the player relies on the spin on the ball which gathers as it runs towards the hoop. The softer the stroke, the more spin. This approach also leaves room for greater accuracy in getting the ball to stop exactly where needed on the other side of the hoop.

When the balls go off the court they must be brought back onto 'the yardline'. This is an imaginary line which runs all round the court one yard in from the painted boundary lines. Once a ball goes over the boundary, it is brought back into play by placing it on the yardline. Most players do this by 'measuring in' a mallet's length from the boundary line and always before the next player takes his turn. If the ball stops between the imaginary yardline and the boundary line, it is also placed back on at a yard's length – unless it is the striker's ball which has gone off after a roquet. When the ball goes off at the corner, it is replaced by measuring in from each boundary line of the angle to find the corner spot.

'Wiring' is the croquet equivalent of being snookered and it is always wise to try to leave the game in such a way that it is difficult for the opponent to 'get the innings' and take over play. This, if you like, is the sophisticated version of putting a ball amidst the rhododendrons though the main object of wiring, or 'cross-pegging' the opponent is not so much to delay him as to make things easier for yourself at the next stage of play.

Once a ball has run all the hoops in both directions and thus scored twelve points, it becomes a 'rover' and can be pegged out – but only when the partner ball has also run the hoops. The exception to this is when one of the opponent's balls has also completed its course through the hoops and is also a rover, in which case you can use your ball to peg it out.

The temptation to remove an opponent's ball is often irresistible. It leaves the striker with a feeling of superiority that can sometimes be fatal. John Solomon, devotes three pages to the question in his book *Croquet* (Batsford, 1966, paperback edition A & C Black, 1989) and comes to no firm conclusion at the end though he does offer the advice never to peg out an opponent when his partner ball is near the end of the game and for rover and to always peg him out if his other ball is left earlier in the game at hoop three back or before.

How to peg out is another matter. Most top class players will use the croquet stroke to firmly peg out both balls. Great care is taken in lining up the balls correctly and then striking firmly against the peg.

Croquet is certainly not the simple pastime that it is often imagined to be. It is a highly scientific game with its own precise terminology and a wide variety of strokes. The way that these can be played and the tactical decisions that face a player are almost infinite.

Watching a game of advanced croquet, the newcomer will be surprised to see the players doing the unexpected. For example, they will stop making hoops and prepare a 'leave' to let their opponent in when it seems that they could easily have continued to score more points. When they leave the balls 'joined up' on the yardline, they will leave them further apart than a beginner or even an intermediate player might consider safe. Once or twice during the game they will take a 'lift' (see p. 139) and pick up the ball and play it from the baulk lines at the beginning of their turn when it is not even wired. Finally, they will constantly talk about 'TPs' or triple peels. These have become such a familiar part of the terminology of contemporary association croquet that although described in more detail later, they are worth a mention straight away. Spectators of the game at any of the top tournaments will certainly see triple peels in action and they are often included in the final score, which may look like this: +26TP.

There are many variations on peeling – including straight peels, standard peels, Irish peels (a stroke rather than a tactic which simply involves croqueting both balls through the same hoop), and the triple peel on opponent (which involves pegging out one of the opponent's balls). In general, triple peels belong to the realms of advanced play in which laws were specially designed to prevent one side walking off with the game too easily.

Unlike snooker, croquet players do not 'concede' when they are far behind in the game. The unpredictable is always waiting to happen and in croquet, no game is ever lost until the other player has won. In 1987, Mark Avery spent seventy-five minutes sitting on the sidelines while Stephen Mulliner forged a lead in the Open Championships. When Avery's turn finally came he eventually went on to win the match and his patience was rewarded.

Nor do association players stop when it rains! Garden players may prefer to appear when there isn't a cloud in the sky but official tournaments are only postponed when the courts can be accurately described as 'waterlogged'. Such circumstances make for some peculiar styles of dress. Wellington boots and shorts topped by a sou'wester have even been favoured by some and the pages of the magazine of the Croquet Association are filled with recommendations for ingenious outfits that promise to keep out the wet and the condensation. One correspondent to the magazine described a tournament in Eastbourne where driving wind and rain made play so uncomfortable that completing a game was 'more a matter of endurance than skill'. The writer's main concern seems to have been the effect this spectacle had on the casual observer as he went on to report anxiously that he had heard several scathing comments from astonished spectators about 'cranks who play croquet in any weather'.

The most common charcteristic amongst players must be their enthusiasm. From the rugged lawns of a small country garden to the sleek rolling greensward set for a tournament, croquet excites a keen response from its protagonists which borders on the euphoric. An article in the April 1926 edition of the gazette provides an early example of this which most players today would still find valid.

'Few who take to croquet and follow up their choice with conscientious practice in the mastery of its rudiments ever repent afterwards of their decision. From its inherent resemblance to billiards, croquet may be considered as a game of the indoor type; yet it is played in the open air and thus combines the advantages of both indoor and outdoor sport. It affords a modicum of exercise with reasonable bodily exertion; yet it demands neither hard training nor strenuous physical effort. Croquet may be learnt, played and enjoyed by persons of almost every age and of either sex, the average proficiency of women-players being not much inferior to that of men – for both sexes it is unquestionably the most companionable of outdoor games. It may even be played and enjoyed by those who are physically disabled.

'The game is sufficiently scientific, as witness a number of books on its tactics, and yet to the average intelligence, it is not so difficult to master . . . (it) demands a so-called "straight" eye, a steady aim, correct stance, complete control of the nerves and mastery of mind over body.

'It is not a game exclusively for elderly maiden ladies, shy curates or young children . . . real croquet is not the game as played at occasional garden parties or some unregistered clubs or in small back gardens with wooden balls, toy mallets, no boundaries, go-as-you-please conditions and "cheat all you can!"'

Even then, it seems that croquet had a mixed reputation. Throughout the years it has had little chance to shake its 'vicious' image. Few magazine or newspaper features can resist a reference to the old cliché and in a novel of the Sixties it was even taken to the ultimate and one of the characters was murdered with a mallet!

Croquet's unfortunate reputation, owes much to its early days in England because when Lewis Carroll wrote his famous description of Alice's game, he was making fun of an aimless social pastime. Yet only a year after Carroll's words were published, the founding father of modern croquet began a series of articles in *The Field* which set out the basics of modern tactics and elevated croquet to a science.

Since then, croquet literature has been greatly increased by collections of books on tactics. Some of these volumes are exceedingly slim and appear to deal more with technique – style, stance and rhythm – than with tactics. Others are designed like the layout of a military campaign. They bristle with complicated diagrams, bombard the reader with technical know-how and all too often, are incomprehensible to all but the most seasoned campaigner.

133

The player who perseveres and arms himself with this heavy artillery often finds that on the actual field of battle, things are not at all as they appear to be in the books. The 'standard tactical shot' soon becomes a meaningless phrase. One of the greatest croquet tacticians of all time, E. P. C. Cotter, summed the matter up by saying that in tactics 'we are not dealing with the absolute but with what is purely relative'.

Tactics are not a code-book to the game of croquet any more than they are to any other sport. Ask Nick Faldo why he played a particular style of shot at a certain hole and he probably will not remember, or if he does, will explain it in terms of its relevance at that particular time. In other words, tactics are dictated by the state of the game which in turn depends upon the calibre of the opponent and the level of his skill in relation to one's own. It is the 'harmonious association of powers' that usually wins the day – as any student of Clausewitz is well aware.

Advanced tactics are very much in vogue today amongst young croquet players. The making of difficult 'leaves' or the use of tactics to tip the psychological balance in an apparently uneven match, has achieved 'state-of-the-art' importance. One has only to look at recent editions of the Croquet Association's magazine, written and edited by players to see how 'tactical' match reporting has become. Each move is recorded and analyzed. Gone are the days when a brief report of the results was generally prefaced with a lengthy dissertation on the weather.

In the end, the object of the game remains the same – to get through all the hoops first. The skill involved in working out how best to do so, separates the 'A Class' player from the rest of the field. Croquet is often compared to chess in the need to 'plan moves ahead'. But unlike chess which is an 'either turn' game, croquet need have no intervening moves so there is nothing to prevent a player working out as many moves ahead as he likes. John Solomon has said he often found himself planning up to nineteen moves ahead. A top player can certainly make some sixty or seventy different shots in a single break.

Good tactics are inventive. They rely on adapting a thorough knowledge of standard moves to a particular situation which takes into account personal ability, the opponent's ability and also, to a lesser degree perhaps, the state of the battlefield. In general, British players are spoilt by the standard of championship lawns. A beautifully cut stretch of grass allows much more finesse in shot-making. The most a player is likely to encounter by way of 'obstruction' on a Hurlingham lawn, is a fallen leaf.

This is just one small but significant difference in the quality of play at tournament level and that which most of us endure (and enjoy) on private lawns. A championship lawn is flat and smooth as a billiard table and it is the first great treat in store for the player who progresses out of the garden, into association croquet.

The higher a player gets in the game, the more he will realize that there is a tremendous amount to learn in croquet tactics – far more than can be contained in a single chapter and more, even, than is successfully covered in most books on the subject. (Two of the best are still John Solomon's *Croquet* and E. P. C. Cotter's *Tackle Croquet This Way*. The latter of which is sadly out of print at present.)

To return to Clausewitz, much of the means of success will depend on such 'unlearnable' elements as resolution and what the Prussian military philosopher referred to as *coup d'oeil* – 'an intellect which, even in the midst of intense obscurity, is not without some traces of inner light, which lead to the truth and then the courage to follow this faint light'. In other words, the ability to decide swiftly upon the right point of attack.

How to Win

To begin the long ascent to this sublime level, every player needs a modicum of tactical know-how. A few fundamentals on different types of shot and how to play them, were covered earlier. The rest of this chapter offers the beginner a little more.

Basic Croquet Tactics

Basic tactics can be described as having the following three objectives: getting the innings, going for the break and planning the leave. Let's take a look at each in turn.

GETTING THE INNINGS

The player who has the innings controls the game. The opponent can do nothing except hope that at some time, the in-player will miss a shot and 'break-down', or that he will decide to end his turn and leave the balls in such a position that it allows the opponent to recover the innings for himself (or, if this isn't possible, to impede the progress of the in-player in the hope that he will eventually break down himself).

The in-player meanwhile has one objective in mind: To get on and finish the game as quickly as possible. Doing this usually means setting up a break.

GOING FOR THE BREAK

'Four-ball breaks' were loosely described earlier. To return to the subject, a 'break' describes a turn in which more than one hoop is made. The most common is the four-ball break, using all the balls, strategically set out, to make as many hoops as possible. Three-ball breaks and two-ball breaks are self-explanatory and obviously more difficult as they leave the player with progressively fewer balls to manoeuvre. In essence, the four-ball break seems simple. The difficulty (and the skill) lies in picking up the break and then, in keeping it going. Very rarely do the balls appear neatly laid out by the hoops in text-book position. The process of arranging them thus, involves a series of shots which the wise player will apply himself to individually. The technique is similar to snooker in that a player can effect top spin on the ball (with a roll), back spin (with a stop shot) and angle the balls with split shots. Other important elements in making a break include accuracy in shooting, hitting a rush and precise action around the hoops. Accurate shooting depends on a number of factors, among them, good swing and rhythm in pushing the mallet forward strongly with the arms, controlled stance and accurate lining up of the ball to be struck with the target and, finally, a certain degree of psychological persuasion. Many players say it helps to believe that you really can hit the target ball and to 'will' it to grow large enough to make it impossible to miss.

The principle of breaks is quite straightforward. In order to make the hoop easily, it helps to play the preceding stroke, or approach shot, from as close as possible. As such, players talk a great deal about 'taking position' and 'making a tidy hoop'. The very best will demonstrate an extraordinary delicacy of touch in manoeuvring their ball to within a few inches of the hoop so that there is no risk involved in knocking it through – particularly important in competition level where the hoops are usually 'narrowed' to allow minimum clearance of the ball. Breaks help the player to position the balls so that it is easy to 'pot' them.

Having made the hoop, the object is to immediately proceed to make the next. The process is made infinitely easier if there is already another ball waiting beside that hoop. To make this possible, the croquet player sends out a 'pioneer' ball to the next hoop but one. This lies ready to help the player make that hoop when he gets to it..In addition, the fourth ball is used as a 'pivot', and is usually positioned in the middle of the court so that it can be 'picked up' with a croquet stroke and used to shorten the distance between pioneers. The natural ratio of distance travelled by balls in a croquet stroke is three to one. By using the pivot ball as a half-way stage to where he wants to play his shots, the croquet player can reduce the distance he is required to play the shots across the court.

At each stage of this process, a miss or a bad approach to a hoop can make the whole thing disintegrate but the over-cautious player will never get very far. Good croquet is attacking croquet and a good player will look to construct a break as soon possible.

Sometimes it is not possible. There may be no realistic opportunity to set up a break. Or, the break which is in progress may suddenly go wrong. In both cases, the important point is not to leave an easy break for the in-coming opponent.

PLANNING THE LEAVE

Once he recognizes his turn is coming to an end, a good player will begin to plan his leave. This involves placing the balls in such a way that causes maximum difficulty for his partner to hit either of them and yet makes it quite easy for himself to pick up the innings again should his opponent fail to keep it and he soon gets another turn.

The 'controlled' leave is highly prized by advanced players though some find the degree of care with which a difficult leave may be set up to be rather excessive. It can be a complicated affair but basically it consists of making sure the last two strokes of a particular turn consist of a croquet stroke and its continuation shot. The croquet stroke, usually a take-off, returns the striker's ball to its partner, a process often referred to as 'joining up'. The final stroke is used to position the ball at close range.

Players will sometimes take considerable time arranging the position of this final shot, leaving the ball close enough to its partner to ensure an easy hit next turn but not so close that it gives the opponent a 'double target' to aim at. Working backwards, a player preparing a leave will have already ensured that, as far as possible, the opponent is left separated and far enough away to constitute a minimum of threat to himself.

A great deal of 'working backwards' goes on in croquet tactics, especially in constructing a break. A player needs to work back from his objective – making all the hoops – to the best way of getting into position to do so. It isn't just a matter of progressing through a set of standard moves, but of rapidly assessing a set of prevailing conditions and working out how to turn them to advantage. Top tactics are inventive, it is that which makes them so interesting. An example might help to illustrate the point.

In the first world championships at Hurlingham, David Openshaw met up with Stephen Mulliner in the quarter finals. Both are experienced players but their approach to the game is quite different. Mulliner has a quick, almost aggressive line of attack. Openshaw's approach is generally more methodical but nonetheless, relentless.

On this occasion, Openshaw was ahead in the first game of three until he missed a long shot at the peg, leaving Mulliner to pick up a three-ball break and steal the game by a mere two points. The second game began somewhat slowly and remained unimpressive until Mulliner was left with one ball for the peg and his other next to it. Openshaw was separated in the first and fourth corners with one clip on four-back and the other on the second hoop. He shot well, hitting across the court to strike his partner ball, then played a split shot to send it to the third hoop, giving himself a rush to the second. He then proceeded to play a three-ball break against time which, as the minutes ticked away, the time-keeper started to call out. Openshaw pushed on, making hoops to the cry of 'four minutes' at four-back, 'one and a half minutes' after rover until he finished his turn with a mere twenty-five seconds to spare. Mulliner cornered to give himself another shot but now that time had been called, Openshaw was able to amble his way slowly through to victory. Because of poor light, the deciding game was then held over to the next day. Openshaw used the psychological advantage he had earned the day before and went on to win the match.

Aficionados of the science of croquet tactics may not agree that this occasion demonstrated anything out of the ordinary. At times, the action seemed either bogged down or lacking in great finesse but Openshaw succeeded in turning defeat into victory. An indifferent middle game against a formidable opponent had been played out on difficult ground, parched dry by an extraordinary week of sunshine, and under tense conditions. His tactics had not relied on any one particular element but on a subtle approach to the whole game which made the most of his own relative mental strength.

First-class players are not expected to 'break down' once they get the innings. They will usually only stop making hoops when they have reached four-back because they do not want to give a 'contact' shot to their opponent.

Law 23 of *advanced singles play* states that if a player's ball 'has scored both 1-back and 4-back in a turn and its partner ball has not scored 1-back before that turn', his opponent is entitled to begin his next turn by lifting either ball and placing it in contact with any of those on the lawn, giving himself a croquet stroke.

This law for *level play*, that is, play between two lowest handicapped players, grew from a series of attempts to prevent players completing a game in two turns by simply going round with the first ball, then lying up in the third corner, leaving his opponent one shot of about forty yards as his only chance of getting into the game. If he missed, the opponent then went on with his second ball to finish. It did not always happen so smoothly but it happened often enough for the Reverend Elvey to be the first in the Twenties, to propose a lift shot after 4-back, allowing the opponent the opportunity to pick up either ball and play it from either of the baulk lines.

The effect on the game was quite revolutionary and needless to say, it did not meet with universal approval. It helped deter the first player from going beyond 4-back and also made it harder for him to finish his break. In doing so, it made the game longer but also opened it up.

Most contemporary players will take their first ball round to 4-back, make a good leave and at the next available opportunity (hopefully after his opponent has tried and missed a lift shot), join it with the second, 'backward' ball and end the match with a triple peel, taking both balls through the last three hoops (4-back, penultimate and rover) and pegging them out together.

Triple peels have grown in importance with the refinement of laws on lift and contact as the tactic gives the opponent only one lift shot. Almost more important than mere tactics however, is the 'Triple's' status as the 'trademark' of the expert. It is a means of showing off his ability and the variations involved, including the possibility of further refining the art to play quadruple peels and even sextuples, leaves him with an ever-widening challenge.

The sextuple peel is the equivalent of a 147-break in snooker and is said to have been 'invented' by John Solomon.

Triple peels are not new. The Reverend Elvey wrote in the Forties that 'a modern book on croquet would hardly be complete which ignored the peels'. He added the following useful advice: 'The moment things begin to go wrong, give up all thought of peels; try and restore your ball positions and carry on with the ordinary break.' Peels are probably the most demanding tactic in the game and the serious student will very soon become addicted to them but they are never worth pursuing to the bitter end and at the risk of failing to get to the peg safely.

A triple peel must be played in the same turn for it to count and when played by an expert, it sometimes looks deceptively easy. There is an elegance in the way the 'professional' swings into the triple on the home run, but even then, all sorts of things can go wrong – and often do.

In the finals of the Singles World Championships in 1989, Mark Avery, playing Joe Hogan, soon won position in the first game and played a relaxed round to reach 4-back. He then went on to start a triple and had completed two peels when, for no apparent reason he stuck in 2-back. Despite a brilliant long shot which brought him back into position later in the game, he never really recovered and Hogan was able to win.

Discussing the matter later, Avery commented, 'Croquet isn't like tennis. You can't work out how to beat someone else's game. Instead, you have to focus on your own. For the most part, I don't plan my tactics, when I'm on good form I like to rely on my shooting, then the rest of the game usually just comes along.'

The beginner, however, cannot rely on his game to just 'come along'. He has to work hard at it and fight for every point against a player of greater ability. Fortunately, croquet has a very effective handicap system which helps him to do just that.

Unlike most games, although a croquet player has a fixed handicap which is reduced as he improves, he does not play off this handicap but the difference between his own and that of his opponent. The system has nothing to do with points as in tennis, or strokes as in golf, but simply consists of giving the higher handicapped player a number of free turns. These are called 'bisques' and are represented by a series of short, white sticks. Nobody knows the origin of the term though the

French *faire bisquer quelqu'un* means to drop them in the soup – which may, or may not, have some relevance.

Handicaps range from –2, the best, to 18, the official figure for beginners which some clubs extend upwards to 24 or sometimes even higher. The system works by offering a player a number of free turns to make up the difference between his handicap and that of his opponent. For example, if his opponent is a ten and he has a handicap of eight, he gives his opponent two bisques – or two free turns. Likewise, if a 15 plays a seven, the 15 receives eight bisques and so on. The bisques are lined up along one edge of the lawn, stuck into the ground and as each free turn is used they are pulled up, usually by the opponent. Half-bisques, restricted free turns in which the player can roquet all the other balls but cannot score points, are represented by shorter sticks.

The application of this rather extraordinary system has often caused debate in the croquet world. There are those who feel that a system which allows two people with a higher handicap or 'long bisquers' as they are called, to play against each other on level terms and, consequently, on the same sort of basis as top players in top events, makes a mockery of the whole idea of handicapping. Worse, it makes it almost impossible for two players of near ability to have a decent game against each other. For example, if two tens play each other, neither side is allowed any bisques and the game can often become stymied in a series of defensive moves.

One way to solve this situation would be to allow each player to take his or her full complement of bisques. So both ten players would be entitled to ten bisques, a ten playing an eight would have ten bisques while his opponent had eight – and so on.

Solomon took up the matter in his book *Croquet* in 1966. Changing the system to allow each player to take bisques would, he thought, enable them to 'get on with the game instead of scraping around for hours with little effective or constructive play'. Many others have since rallied to the idea, the main opposition to which seems to be that it would require more sticks or 'bisques' than most clubs seem able to furnish!

Even so, the present practice of playing on the handicap difference seems to work tolerably well. It enables newcomers to start off with a temporary handicap which can be quickly reduced once they have been seen in play and, most important, it allows a player of medium ability to take on a much better player and use his free turns to create breaks. Some feel that it is a waste of time for a beginner to arm himself with a 'fence' of bisques against a good player, on the grounds that the psychological element will always defeat the newcomer, no matter how many free turns he has.

That may be true in many cases but pitting ones wits against a really good player has its uses. It can encourage the higher handicap to make proper use of his bisques, not just to make a single hoop, but as progress points towards setting up a better situation on the court. The old adage 'bisques equals breaks' contains more than a grain of truth but in any case, the long bisquer is generally wise to only continue the innings with a bisque, providing he can see the way forward to the next hoop but one.

Writing in a copy of the gazette in 1949, Maurice Reckitt advised 'by far the most formidable use of bisques is for the purpose of attack, and the more bisques you are receiving, the more true this is. Use your bisques (or better still, half-bisques) at the earliest opportunity to establish a break and then go ahead and use more if necessary to make it.'

The key words here are 'make it'. It is always wiser to retreat in orderly fashion than to continue to throw away points in an effort to retrieve a situation that has completely broken down.

Bisques can be used at any time during the game after an ordinary turn. Say for example, a player has succeeded in setting up a likely looking break with pioneer and pivot balls in position, but then misses the ball he needs to croquet to make his next hoop. He might well feel that taking a bisque and saving the break, is a worthwhile action. The free turn allows the player to begin all over again. So if he has already roqueted a ball before taking the bisque, he can go back and roquet it again. In effect, the action of taking the bisque is like leaving the court and coming back to begin a whole new turn. Sometimes it is worth taking bisques to rectify single mistakes (like being stuck in a hoop) but in general the experts agree that bisques are best taken as a series of free turns which enable the player to set up an early break and to get ahead in the game. The idea is to take one ball round with one half of the bisques and the other ball round with the other half. For that reason, it is always a good idea to make the better player go first if you win the toss as he then has to play a three-ball break while you, the higher handicap, should always wait until all four balls are in play before using up bisques.

The standard tactic, as has been seen, is to take the bisques early on in the game and use them to establish and maintain four-ball breaks but where the difference between the two players only allows a few bisques in one's favour, it may be advisable to use them more sparingly. In an article on the subject, Professor Bernard Neal recommended keeping one bisque in hand 'to snatch the innings if a crisis arises at the end of the game'.

Early tactics in croquet should concentrate on learning how to set up breaks without having to play difficult strokes. One of the fundamentals of good break play is learning how to make each stroke shorter and easier for yourself while ensuring that anything left for the opponent is to his disadvantage. But croquet is a psychological game and even the best players cannot depend on things always going right. It's a thought worth bearing in mind when everything seems to be going wrong, that at sometime or other, the same has happened to your opponent, however cool and collected he may appear at present, and that there is always the possibility of it happening to him again. The David and Goliath principle has seen many interesting results on the croquet lawn.

The intermediate stage is probably the hardest for most croquet players – and the stage at which most, commonly stick. Solomon refers to it as 'that "difficult" stage'. It comes when a complete newcomer, or a former garden player has learnt the fundamentals of the association game and watched a few 'A Class' players at work. He knows what he wants to do but somehow, once on the lawn, the application escapes him. The best way to uncork potential at this level is to enrol in one of the Croquet Association's coaching courses. These generally last two days and cover all the principles of good play. Here are a few examples:

1 Use bisques early in the game to establish breaks and look for 'high profit' situations where a single bisque can earn several points.

2 Try not to leave the opponent free shots and doubles.

3 Be aware of the danger of wiring your opponent and giving away a lift unless he has pegged out one ball when the two-ball player should look for opportunities to wire.

4 Play peels with a firm grip, taking care not to twist the mallet when playing the stop shot.

5 Plan hoop approaches to get a useful rush after making the hoop.

6 Play thick take-off shots with a firm straight swing and plenty of follow through.

7 Use bisques to help tidy up disintegrating breaks.

8 Use rushes to shorten the distance between strokes and make croquet strokes easier.

9 Keep the pivot ball mobile, so as to avoid long take-off shots.

10 Know the laws of the game. This gives confidence and could help earn victory.

THE DILEMMA
'Gentlemen versus Players'

More than a hundred years of history has done little to subdue the passion of the croquet player. He (and she) is still a 'concerned' human being, given to full and frequent expression in print about such important matters as a point of difference over roquets or the price of entry to tournaments. The smallest change to tradition produces the rallying cry, 'The future of our game is at risk.' Since first publication in 1904, the Croquet Gazette has provided a forum for debate and a vital means of keeping all the members of the association in touch. Nowadays, simply called *Croquet*, it is still referred to by many of its readers as 'the gazette' and has provided a link between the rather elevated world of the Council and the more mundane proceedings in the annual life of the clubs. Results of tournaments are traditionally reported in the gazette, to a greater or lesser degree, depending on the mood of the moment, but this is only a small part of its role.

All life is revealed in the gazette, and all passing of life for it has been another tradition to record the deaths of members. These obituaries make absorbing reading. Often revealing more in what has been left out than what has been put in, they form potted histories of many of croquet's best loved characters and also provide a keen insight into the changing times of the croquet world.

Producing such a record has been a costly process at times and the size of issues has shrunk or expanded in response to financial pressure. The name of the magazine has been changed almost as many times as its editor, to suit the prevailing fashion.

Various editors have promoted different styles. Some preferred the dry, documented method of simply filling the pages with tournament results. Others have tried to encourage features covering a variety of topics including coaching courses, travel, tactics, history and even short story competitions. In 1972, the editorial took the bold step of sending out a questionnaire with the April edition. Two-thirds of those who replied stated they would prefer less space devoted to tournament results and over half asked for shorter reports. The replies reflected the widely held belief that the gazette appeared to devote more space to successful players in major tournaments at the expense of the majority of its subscribers who have little opportunity to attend these events. The centre seemed self-absorbed.

Early copies of the gazette were jolly affairs. Although they did not have many photographs, they were filled with enticing advertisements, many of them from hotels offering croquet tournaments. The size of the magazine was larger, allowing for frequent digression in the long reports of tournaments to include anecdotes about various participants and occasionally, even notes of an ornithological nature. 'A player busy with a break looked up and saw a cuckoo sitting on the second hoop, surely a rare occurrence on a croquet lawn during a game.' Then as now, the weather preoccupied many contributors and the correspondence column was a major feature. *Croquet* has the sort of reader reaction that most national newspaper editors fantasize about. Nothing escapes the subscribers scrutiny and down the years, letters have poured in on subjects of every description from points of croquet law to designs for the cover of the magazine itself.

Occasionally, a matter of 'national importance' still works its way to the top of the pile. In the last few years, there have been a surprising number of them, mostly related to promoting the game and the associated questions of 'professionalism' and sponsorship.

Many of croquet's devotees, young and old, are appalled at the thought of money 'tainting' their sport. For them, sponsorship smacks of 'nasty commercialism', the sort of unpleasant media attention that beams down upon tennis, attracting television and crowds of people. If one could guarantee that the latter were the passive sort, like snooker or golf supporters generally are, this might not seem so bad but there is a fear that croquet might become like cricket.

Others see sponsorship as the only means of expansion and growth in croquet. Tournaments cost money. Individual clubs are loath to increase subscriptions and the Croquet Association can hope for little extra income from elsewhere. Sponsorship is one of the few ways of earning the sport the self-sufficiency it needs, especially while croquet continues to expand its international network and more tournaments are held abroad.

So far, croquet's sponsorship has mostly been of an alcoholic nature. Gin, lager and wine substances have all been poured into the game and their contribution gratefully soaked up – in more ways than one. In return, the sponsors have got very little. No television coverage and a miniscule amount of notice from the press. Most sponsors settle for a few good lunches at Hurlingham and the dubious publicity coup of scooping the back page of *Croquet* magazine. At least one seemed less than enthusiastic with the arrangement and announced that it would not be renewing its sponsorship unless some sort of TV coverage was guaranteed. Meanwhile, though craving attention, croquet seemed prepared to hinder its own progress by continuing its long-established tradition of internal squabbling.

In 1983, the Council considered a report by the Sponsorship Committee which eloquently argued in favour of televizing golf croquet. Golf croquet is rather like putting – hence its name. It is played alternately and a turn consists of only one stroke. The aim of the game is to be the first through the hoops but unlike association croquet, the balls are played in order of colour and the croquet stroke is not used. For many, this latter point is very important and they argue that because there is no croquet stroke, it really cannot be called croquet at all.

However, the game seems ideally suited to television because it is interactive, offers a variety of shots, takes only an average of about twenty-five minutes to complete and allows coverage of close play around the hoops. In contrast, association croquet can be a one-sided affair, the average game takes a couple of hours and the business of setting up and making breaks encompasses a large area and is not always instantly comprehensible to the casual viewer.

All this, and much more was set out in the Sponsorship Committee's report. In addition the report argued that to gain sponsorship, croquet needed to be 'recognized generally to be reasonably serious, skilful and worthwhile'. Television coverage was a commercial fact of life and as this in turn was divided into 'specialist' and 'entertainment' games, then croquet must do its best to entertain. Golf croquet, it was concluded, came closest to achieving this aim and was therefore 'easily the most suitable form of croquet for television'.

Uproar greeted the report. The gazette bristled with letters of indignation. 'Council seems to be selling its birthright for a mess of pottage,' protested one correspondent. 'We who play this magnificent game of croquet should guard the name jealously,' wrote another, adding that the name should not be used 'for any inferior game which lacks its unique qualities'. Because of a ruling that Council members should not put a contrary motion before other members, one official felt the need to resign as he intended 'to oppose this policy (of televizing golf croquet) with all the vehemence I can command'.

The argument that raged was centred around the question of whether or not golf croquet was sufficiently worthy and representative of croquet in general to be televized. One side believed it was, the other, that croquet did not wish to be represented by this 'relatively foolish game'. Deep down however, one suspects that there were many who feared the intrusion of television and the great wide world into any form of croquet and hid their prejudice behind defence of the association game. Meanwhile, the controversy and emotion that the matter aroused equalled anything that had happened during the political in-fighting of Walter Jones Whitmore's day.

In the end, those opposed to publicizing golf croquet won the day. At the Annual General Meeting in April 1984, a motion was put forward 'That Council's decision of 29 October 1983 to seek sponsorship for golf croquet be reversed'. It went on to demand that Council be prevented from further attempts to attract either sponsorship or publicity for golf croquet without the permission of the association's members taken at a general meeting. The motion was carried – by two votes. Thirty-six voted for and thirty-four against, numbers which indicated the depth of feeling as this was an unusually large turnout at Hurlingham for an AGM.

A second motion, to change the name of golf croquet to 'Hoop Golf', was decisively defeated. Other suggestions for a new name, including that of 'Hoopball' (as in netball, basketball etc.) were also dismissed. The fact that it was neither golf, nor croquet, did not change its character for many people and there were still plenty who thought that when played seriously, 'Golf Croquet is a good game and plays an important part in a club socially'. Keith Wylie, who was also quoted in golf croquet's defence (though it appears he actually wrote the article some time prior to this particular debate) added that he thought that just as much skill was required to play golf croquet as for the association game and that 'to suggest otherwise is to display one's ignorance'.

The real point of the debate had been obscured in all this commotion. It was not the value of golf croquet which was in contention but the belief that the game was about to be changed out of all recognition by those who wanted to see things organized on a more commercial basis.

The Sponsorship Committee retired to fight another day and it was not long before the subject was to resurface in a slightly different form. Meanwhile, they must surely have been dejected at the attitude of those who felt moved to remark that 'Croquet is too subtle and complex to achieve general popularity, and all efforts to do that must surely fail'.

Television finally happened in 1986. To avoid further consternation in the ranks, a form of 'short croquet' was decided upon. Lionel Wharrad, the then Chairman, claims that it was his invention, specifically designed to 'bring the croquet lawn into frame'.

Short croquet uses all the rules of association croquet but the balls only go round the hoops once for a 14-point game and the lawn is effectively half-size. The television event was to be called the Nation's Trophy and three players from four teams (England, Scotland, Ireland and Wales) would compete against each other to produce one supremo. A total of eight hours coverage was to appear on Granada. The Royal Bank of Scotland gallantly offered sponsorship and the stage seemed set for croquet to step into the floodlights. Sadly, the nation remained unmoved by the event. For a start, the programmes were only shown to viewers in the north-east. Unaware of the immense honour being bestowed on them, these viewers responded rather warily with average viewing figures of 285,000 for the eleven programmes, the highest figures for an individual programme being for the screening on Wednesday afternoon at 5.15!

In general, the audience's reaction to the broadcasts seems to have been one of total bemusement. But if the great British public were unexcited, the croquet world was in a twitter. 'We've been on TV!' cried a delighted editorial in the gazette while John Walters, writing up his report with his usual attention to detail, concentrated on the real

issues at hand and referred for the most part to meals at Pizzaland and
the inability to get prompt service in the local hotel bar.

Meanwhile, croquet's annual 'round of drinks' continued. Despite
the fact that once they had signed on a sponsor, the administration
seemed to forget all about them, the financial arrangement appeared
satisfactory to both sides. To date, sponsorship of croquet has come
remarkably cheap. Three years at Hurlingham can cost a sponsor less
than half the outlay for a single day of polo on Smith's lawn. Mutterings
about 'quality' and 'appropriateness' of sponsors have long since
dwindled to nothing as the association has become increasingly open to
offers, be it from lawn mower manufacturers or the makers of butter.
An American airline sponsored the first singles World Championships
and also flew Great Britain and Ireland's team in early 1990 to the
MacRobertson Test in the antipodes. Despite the fact that the journey
was so long the players passed beyond mere jet-lag into a totally
different mind-zone and that luggage, including precious mallets, was
mislaid, everyone, especially the players, was pathetically grateful.
Croquet's administration, it seems, was prepared to take up almost any
offer of a bit of cash.

Until recently, however, the players themselves might not do
anything at all. For years, the level of prize money remained fixed at a
derisory £25. Gradually it became obvious that the rising cost of
entering a tournament – in terms of fees, travel, and when necessary,
overnight accommodation, far outweighed any 'profit' the winner
might make. In addition, the prizes that the more generous sponsors
chose to bestow on croquet were increasingly worth more than £25. In
fact, croquet prizes had once been very valuable indeed. Lillie records
that the prizes for the early tournaments in England included a pair of
marble vases, a silver claret jug and 'a colt, only seventeen years of
age'. A contemporary player would expect to be far less fortunate and
could easily walk away from a tournament several pounds out of pocket
but having been entrusted with a cup bearing an insurance value of
thousands of pounds. (Croquet's collection of trophies is impressive
but attempts to encourage greater care of them, such as locking them
up in bank vaults for most of the year have been vetoed by members
who feel they should either be enjoyed – or sold.)

Recognizing that something had to be done, a few players took the
matter quietly into their own hands. Money, it seemed, could be
legitimately earned by coaching, but even this was not without its

problems. In the late Eighties, Mark Avery became something of a croquet 'test case'. He was offered a coaching job in the USA and, being keen to spend more time playing croquet than working as a building site surveyor in Ipswich, he accepted. It seemed straightforward enough but for once, the media thought it had found a story. The cry went up – 'Croquet goes professional'. It was enough to provoke another fusillade of letters to the magazine. The Croquet Council, which has always taken a dim view of players pocketing profit in the past, took this particular storm with remarkable calm, perhaps because several of its members were not unsympathetic to the idea that coaching was no bad thing and moderate amounts of money in remuneration were no bad thing either. In the end, Avery's career as a transcontinental coach was, on this occasion, short-lived. The work he had been 'promised' never quite materialized and he soon returned to play in England. Meanwhile, the question of prize money had been hotly debated amongst the association membership and it was finally agreed to raise the ceiling for prize money from £25 to £2,000 (plus expenses). This was real progress, not least because the exclusion of 'professionals' from tournaments was also revised in that it was henceforth to be left to the discretion of tournament organizers rather than made compulsory.

Some people felt it was all a storm in a teacup. Professionalism, they argued, could never be a real threat to British croquet. Few players competing in the British season could ever hope to clear £2,000 and only those lucky enough to play abroad could collect anything approaching this amount of money, and then probably only during play in America.

Here, as chapter two has shown, the croquet scene is very different. The American game makes money and the USCA is run as a profit-making organization. In recent years they have established a very comfortable annual turnover and they actively promote the game as a business, not only by encouraging new members and clubs but with celebrity events and high-yielding tournaments where eager competitors can be charged £50 or more for the privilege of taking part. But already, there are rumblings that the growing commercial spirit amongst players is having an adverse effect on the game.

In 1988, some thirteen prize money events were held in the USA and Canada, compared to only one major event the year before. The total prize money was $75,350 as opposed to $15,000 in 1987, and the top money winner was a Canadian, Reid Fleming, who collected a total of $6,775 from five tournaments. In 1989, two large prize money events took place. These were the Croquet Masters, a singles tournament which was played in Georgia in April and the Domaine Mumm Classic, a doubles tournament held at Meadowood Resort, St Helena, California, in August. The total purse for the former was $25,000 with $30,000 being offered for the Domaine Mumm. Mark Avery and Reid Fleming won the latter, taking the top prize of $8,000 beating Fred Rogerson of Ireland and Jerry Stark of America into second place with a prize of $5,000. This sum alone more than equalled Fred Rogerson's entire 'earnings' from American croquet the year before. The organizers of the Domaine Mumm cooperated with the USCA to ensure that the tournament was scheduled around, rather than in competition with the main national events of the season, thus allowing top players to enter both. Other promoters were less scrupulous and 'play for pay' began to raise problems.

Several of America's top players declined to take part in the Solomon Trophy (an annual international tournament between Britain and the USA which is held alternately in America and England) because they preferred to keep themselves free for a high-stakes professionally-promoted event, scheduled to take place a week before, and in direct competition with the Solomon Trophy. The Masters (which ended its inaugural year 'entangled in a maze of legal and other issues') was also scheduled right after the National Club Team Championships which prompted some players to opt out of the national competition in favour of 'play for pay'.

Members of the USCA found themselves struggling to keep control of their game, not only against the 'greed is good' attitude of those more interested in earning money than playing in their country's team but also from voracious croquet promoters wanting to start independent croquet companies for profit. The latter refused to work within the national governing body of the sport and to cooperate on the scheduling of tournaments.

All this prompted one American player to gloomily conclude that 'the opportunity to play for money elicits an inherent materialism'. It was food for thought for those in Britain who had looked to the American game as a model on which to base the future organization of their own.

Meanwhile, back in the 'Old Country', the debate on 'professionalism' was slowly warming up. After a very honourable eight years, Coles, the estate agents, had decided to withdraw sponsorship from the Western Championships usually held at Cheltenham. A firm of investment advisors stepped into the breach but Cheltenham Club decided to take this opportunity to make the event Britain's first professional tournament. Entry fees were hiked up to pay for cash prizes totalling around £530 and in defence of its action, Cheltenham announced that it hoped by these means to make the financing of the tournament independent of sponsorship and to thus secure its future 'even it we fail to obtain commercial support'.

As could be expected, the matter was instantly taken up in the correspondence page of *Croquet*. A member from Bristol wrote to say that it was his belief that the opportunity to win 'a substantial cheque' could only 'introduce thoroughly undesirable elements into the game'. Another commented that as there seemed to be a slim chance of people 'queueing at the turnstiles' to see croquet, 'why chance the introduction of "needle" by getting players to compete for substantial sums of their own money?' (raised by increasing entry fees) Into the forefront of the fray strode the impressive figure of Richard Hilditch who saw this as the 'first step down the slippery slope to professionalism' and called upon the top fifty players (those most likely to gain entry) to join him in a boycott of the event. His rallying cry went largely unheeded though it provoked Council member Stephen Mulliner to express his concern that 'the tactics of the picket line are attempting to invade the world of croquet'.

Mulliner pointed out that both the Australian Croquet Association and the New Zealand Croquet Council had recently abolished any distinction between amateurs and professionals and argued that 'a corps of professional coaches would be a significant benefit to players and clubs alike'. In this he was undoubtedly correct. As the sport gains popularity, the demand for coaching increases and to date, it has been answered by unpaid volunteers. However, the idea of a body of paid coaches seems as remote as that of a full-time professional staff in any other area of croquet's increasingly wide administration. Already in recent years, costs have risen as posts that have readily been filled on a voluntary basis in the past become paid jobs. More events and more international tournaments have also meant more work and more money. By 1900, the International Committee were pushing up a budget deficit and the raising of entry fees for CA events (including doubling the entry fee for the World Championships) seemed unlikely to plug the widening hole.

'Professionalism' of another kind was getting a grip on the association's finances as it became increasingly obvious that recruiting the services of unpaid volunteers who had always supported the game in the past was becoming more difficult.

As croquet endeavoured to become more 'organized' and as the number of international tournaments mushroomed, the strain on the central administration also grew. Increased attention from the press (encouraged as a by-product of sponsorship) seemed to require the appointment of a press officer and more tournaments meant more managers, who were also beginning to look for payment. Several years ago, in 1986 the editor of *Croquet* had addressed the subject and urged members of the association to think about the possible impact of 'professionalism' on croquet and consider what roles professionals, either as players or coaches, should be allowed to take in the game. Not much had been resolved in the interval.

Meanwhile, the game seemed to have produced a sudden glut of good players. These could be divided into the veterans – the vintage collection who had mostly left the lawns to take up residence in the record books; the middle-stagers, many of whom were good though never perhaps brilliant and the newcomers – a collection of young men who breezed into the game like a breath of fresh air.

Already, Stephen Mulliner had tried to put order into the game by establishing a set of national rankings (see p. 108). Complicated to most croquet players and nearly incomprehensible to outsiders, the system was soon regarded with suspicion as players began to fear that these rankings would have a direct influence on any selection committee for forthcoming major events, such as Test matches.

Alternative systems were suggested, including a weighting system which, for example, would make twice as many points available in the World Championships as in other events. The obvious detraction of this was that it left out the humbler events such as weekend provincial club tournaments and gave the vast majority of participants barely a look-in. While discussion on a universal method of ranking continued, the Chairman of the Selection Committee announced that following a Council request for assistance in preparing a British team to play in the1990 Test in New Zealand, the Committee had decided to make its own annual assessment at the start of each season. This was to depend on several factors other than 'current form', including past experience and 'attitude'. The players were placed in four groups (or five as 'Group Three' was divided into two sections). The first group listed (in alphabetical order) those 'with an established reputation in major championships' who would gain automatic selection – at the time this meant Mark Avery, Nigel Aspinall, Stephen Mulliner and David Openshaw. The second group listed those selected on 'current form' and established reputation. Group 3a was to include players who had been in Group 1 or 2 in the past, had now slipped, but were expected to make it back up to Group 2. Group 3b included players who had reached President's Cup standard and 'had given the indication that they might improve to Group 2'. Group 4 was for those who were still struggling to reach President's Cup standard but were expected to do so 'if they continued to improve'.

Altogether, it was a wonderful piece of 'through-the-looking-glass' logic and meant very little to anyone except the handful of players named. The committee, recognizing perhaps that this system blissfully ignored a large number of players, added that it obviously could not name all those with 'an outside chance of selection through some major and unexpected change in form' but that it hoped the list would encourage those who had been named and 'whose form is recognized as improving'. In the end, Test players were chosen from each group but, as in many other sports, selectors seem to be a law unto themselves and their choice was greeted with amazement and an unpleasant degree of 'feeling'. For many, it was a sign that the spirit of things was not at all as relaxed as everyone liked to imagine.

'Anyone who says he plays for fun is a loser. This is a real game and you have to play to win.' This comment by a young player clearly reflects that croquet at association level is no longer an idle pastime. Sponsorship and the desire for more press coverage create a pressure for interest which, in turn, breeds pressure for success. Winning becomes important. Competition between players is intense and the onus on the governing body of croquet to promote this as an active spectator sport means that there can be less emphasis on the game as a gentle and leisurely pastime.

Croquet is now into its second 'three-year plan' funded by the Sports Council. The first began in 1985 with a fanfare of projections, including the appointment of a development officer to oversee the increase of individual membership and of new clubs, to promote regional organizations, to set up a National Coaching Scheme and to encourage publicity and sponsorship and increased media coverage.

Chris Hudson, a member of Bowdon Club in Cheshire who had already been involved in croquet for some fifteen years and was a member of Council, was appointed as development officer. In this position, he has helped bring more change to croquet, in the last five years, than has been seen in the last fifty. By the end of his first 'Three-year Forward Plan', croquet had become an increasingly popular game. The National Coaching Scheme was underway with some two dozen high-grade coaches working with a much larger network of club coaches. The Regional Development, begun in 1982 with appointments for nine Sports Council regions had expanded to a national network of voluntary officers who in turn worked to increase the number of regional federations. Most impressive of all perhaps, was the increase in clubs and membership. When setting out its projections in 1984, the proponents of the 'Forward Plan' modestly envisaged an increase of ten new clubs a year. In fact, they more than doubled their expectations, getting an additional sixty-five in the first three years, bringing the number of officially registered clubs to a total of 155.

In addition, membership which had stood at 907 in 1984, soared to over 4,000. Once again, the Forward Plan had more than met its expectations. It had hoped for a mere 1,500 members by the end of 1989.

One of the most laudable efforts at promotion has been the attempt to encourage the playing of croquet in schools. Here, in addition to the association's efforts, the labours of a few dedicated croquet-playing teachers in a handful of schools about the country have produced a remarkable record in a short period of time. In 1986, the Royal Bank of Scotland National School Championships began and to date, has produced a series of winning youngsters who have emerged from the competing teams to give the game a real future.

Perhaps the real triumph of this period however, was the introduction of a Garden Croquet Classic. Played throughout the country in a variety of venues from clubs to country homes, this has been a very worthwhile attempt at uniting the two 'camps' of garden and association croquet. Slowly, it is succeeding in bringing new people into the 'real' game and in spreading the word that croquet can be more than an 'idle pastime'.

For the future of croquet lies beyond Hurlingham and a fistful of top tournaments. Seen from the centre, the view looks limited but from the outside, it is vast. Many members of the Croquet Council are wise enough to realize that the twin sides of croquet, the garden game and the association game must progress together and that the only way forward is via a change of attitude – within the game as much as towards it.

In 1897, Arthur Lillie wrote, 'Through the history of croquet there have been two antagonisms. Garden party croquet has opposed Wimbledon croquet, the man with the baby mallet has fought the man with the large mallet. One group has defined the word "croquet" to mean the relaxation of the idler, an excuse for fashionable folk to meet and converse. The other group, toiling and indefatigable has pronounced it a business. And each has wished not only to conquer but to suppress the other, failing to see that victory meant the death of both.' *Plus ça change* . . .

Today there *is* hope that the two sides of the dilemma can be reconciled. As long as the management and administration of the game remains in the hands of its players it will never, as history has already recorded, lose its true character. And as today's players continue to get younger, and the game grows in popularity, croquet's future looks very bright indeed.

APPENDIX 1
National Register of Official Clubs

(by courtesy of Townsend's Croquet Almanack*)*

A. *Registered Clubs (GB & Ireland)*

1 ALDERMASTON CROQUET CLUB
Aldermaston Croquet Club AWRE, Aldermaston, Reading, Berks.

2 ALL-ENGLAND LAWN TENNIS & CROQUET CLUB
All-England LT & Croquet Club Church Road, Wimbledon, London SW19 5AE

3 ALRESFORD CROQUET CLUB
Alresford Croquet Club 68 Jacklyns Lane, Alresford, Hants SO24 9LH

4 ANCELL TRUST SPORTS CLUB
Ancell Trust Sports Club Croquet Section, Osterley Lane, Stony Stratford, Milton Keynes.

5 ASHBY CROQUET CLUB
Ashby Croquet Club

6 AUCHINCRUIVE CROQUET CLUB
Auchincruive Croquet Club

7 BASINGSTOKE CROQUET CLUB
Basingstoke Croquet Club

8 BATH CROQUET CLUB
Bath Croquet Club Sports Centre, Recreation Ground, Bath, Avon.

9 BEAR OF RODBOROUGH CROQUET CLUB
Bear of Rodborough Croquet Club Bear of Rodborough Hotel, Rodborough Common, Rodborough, Stroud, Glos.

10 BEECHAM PHARAMACEUTICALS (HARLOW) CC
Beecham Pharmaceuticals CC The Pinnacles, Harlow, Essex.

11 BELSAY HALL CROQUET CLUB
Belsay Hall Croquet Club Belsay Hall, Belsay, Northumberland.

12 BENTLEY CROQUET CLUB
Bentley Croquet Club Pilgrims Hall, Bentley, Brentwood, Essex.

13 BEVERLEY CROQUET CLUB
Beverley Croquet Club

14 BOURNEMOUTH CROQUET
CLUB
Bournemouth Croquet Club Seafield
Gardens, Bournemouth, Dorset.

15 BOWDON CROQUET CLUB
Bowdon Croquet Club St Mary's
Road, Bowdon, Cheshire.

16 BRETBY CROQUET CLUB
Bretby Croquet Club N.C.B. R & D
Establishment, Ashby Road, Bretby,
Burton-on-Trent, Staffs.

17 BRISTOL CROQUET CLUB
Bristol Croquet Club Cedar Park,
Stoke Bishop, Bristol BS9 1LW

18 BUDLEIGH SALTERTON LT &
CROQUET CLUB
Budleigh Salterton LT & CC West-
field Close, Upper Stoneborough
Lane, Budleigh Salterton, Devon
EX9 6ST

19 BURNHAM-ON-CROUCH
CROQUET CLUB
Burnham-onCrouch Croquet Club

20 BURY CROQUET CLUB
Bury Croquet Club

21 BURY ST. EDMUNDS &
DISTRICT CROQUET CLUB
Bury St. Edmunds & District CC

22 BUSH CROQUET CLUB
Bush Croquet Club

23 CANUTE CROQUET CLUB
Canute Croquet Club Nuclear Power
Co. (Risley) Ltd. Warrington Road,
Risley, Warrington, Lancs. WA3
6BZ

24 CARRICKMINES CROQUET & LT
CLUB
Carrickmines Croquet & LT Club
Carrickmines, Co. Dublin, Eire.

25 CASSIOBURY CROQUET CLUB
Cassiobury Croquet Club Cassio-
bury Park, Cassiobury Park Avenue,
Watford, Herts.

26 CATERHAM CROQUET CLUB
Caterham Croquet Club Queens
Park, Caterham, Surrey.

27 CHELTENHAM CROQUET CLUB
Cheltenham Croquet Club Old Bath
Road, Cheltenham, Glos. GL53
7DF

28 CHESTER CROQUET CLUB
Chester Croquet Club Westminster
Park, Hough Green, Chester.

29 CHICHESTER CROQUET CLUB
Chichester Croquet Club

30 CIRENCESTER CROQUET CLUB
Cirencester Croquet Club c/o Bing-
ham House, Cirencester, Glos.

31 COAL RESEARCH CROQUET
CLUB
Coal Research Croquet Club British
Coal, Stoke Orchard, Cheltenham,
Glos. GL52 4RZ

32 COLCHESTER CROQUET CLUB
Colchester Croquet Club Ellanore
Road, Colchester, Essex CO3 3UN

33 COLWORTH CROQUET CLUB
Colworth Croquet Club Unilever
Research Laboratories Colworth
House, Shambrook, Bedford MK44
1LQ

34 COMPTON CROQUET CLUB
Compton Croquet Club Saffrons
Sports Club, Compton Place Road,
Eastbourne, E. Sussex.

35 CRANFORD CROQUET CLUB
Cranford Croquet Club 42 Salterton
Road, Exmouth, Devon EX8 2EQ

36 CRAWLEY CROQUET CLUB
Crawley Croquet Club Milton Gardens, Pound Hill, Crawley, W. Sussex.

37 CROMER CROQUET CLUB
Cromer Croquet Club The Tennis Courts, Norwich Road, Cromer, Norwich NR27 OEX

38 CROOME COURT CROQUET CLUB
Croome Court Croquet Club Croome Court, Severn Stoke, Worcester

39 DOWNHAM CROQUET CLUB
Downham Croquet Club Stow Hall, Stow Bardolph, Downham Market, Norfolk.

40 DULWICH SPORTS CLUB LTD
Dulwich Sports Club Ltd Croquet Section, Turney Road, Dulwich, London SE21 7JA

41 DYFFRYN CROQUET CLUB
Dyffryn Croquet Club

42 EALING CROQUET CLUB
Ealing Croquet Club

43 EAST DORSET LT & CROQUET CLUB
East Dorset LT & Croquet Club Salterns Road, Parkstone, Poole, Dorset.

44 EAST RIDING CROQUET CLUB
East Riding Croquet Club Costello Playing Fields, Pickering Road, Hull, Humberside.

45 EDEN PARK CROQUET CLUB
Eden Park Croquet Club Co-op Sports Ground, Balmoral Avenue, Eden Park, Beckenham, Kent.

46 EDGBASTON CROQUET CLUB
Edgbaston Croquet Club Richmond Hill Road, Edgbaston, Birmingham.

47 EDINBURGH CROQUET CLUB
Edinburgh Croquet Club Laurinston Castle and Morningside Park, Edinburgh.

48 ELLESMERE BOWLING, TENNIS & CROQUET CLUB
Ellesmere Bowling, LT & CC Walkden Road, Worsley, Manchester.

49 EMBER SPORTS CLUB
Ember Sports Club The Drive, Ember Lane, Esher, Surrey

50 EXETER CROQUET CLUB
Exeter Croquet Club Princes Park, Exeter, Devon.

51 FYLDE CROQUET CLUB
Fylde Croquet Club Fairhaven Lake, Lytham St. Annes, Lancs.

52 GLASGOW CROQUET CLUB
Glasgow Croquet Club Glasgow Green, Glasgow.

53 GUERNSEY CROQUET CLUB
Guernsey Croquet Club

54 GUILDFORD & GODALMING CROQUET CLUB
Guildford & Godalming CC The Clubhouse, Broadwater, Guildford Road, Godalming, Surrey.

55 HARROGATE CROQUET CLUB
Harrogate Croquet Club Cairn Hotel, Harrogate.

56 HARROW OAK CROQUET CLUB
Harrow Oak Croquet Club Cunningham Park, Hindes Road, Harrow, Middx.

57 HARWELL CROQUET CLUB
Harwell Croquet Club Harwell Research Labs., Harwell, Didcot, Oxon.

58 HARWICH & DOVERCOURT CROQUET CLUB
Harwich & Dovercourt CC The Countryman Club, Marine Parade, Dovercourt, Essex.

59 HAVERING CROQUET CLUB
Havering Croquet Club

60 HELLEDON TENNIS & CROQUET CLUB
Helledon LT & Croquet Club

61 HIGH WYCOMBE CROQUET CLUB
High Wycombe Croquet Club Bassetsbury Manor, Bassetsbury Lane, London Road, High Wycombe, Bucks.

62 HIMLEY CROQUET CLUB
Himley Croquet Club Himley Hall, Dudley, Staffs.

63 HOVE LAWNS CROQUET CLUB
Hove Lawns Croquet Club Sea Front, Hove, E. Sussex.

64 HUNSTANTON CROQUET CLUB
Hunstanton Croquet Club Lynn Road, Hunstanton, Norfolk.

65 HURLINGHAM CLUB
The Hurlingham Club Ranelagh Gardens, London, SW6 3PR

66 IPSWICH & DISTRICT CROQUET CLUB
Ipswich & District Croquet Club Lower Arboretum, Christchurch Avenue, Ipswich, Suffolk.

67 JEALOTTS HILL CROQUET CLUB
Jealotts Hill Croquet Club ICI Plant Protection Div., Jealott's Hill Research, Bracknell, Berks. RG12 6EY

68 JERSEY CROQUET CLUB
Jersey Croquet Club F.B. Fields, Plat Douet Road, St. Helier, Jersey, Channel Islands

69 KENILWORTH LT & CROQUET CLUB
Kenilworth LT & Croquet Club

70 KINGSTON MAURWARD ASSOCIATION CROQUET CLUB
Kingston Maurward ACC

71 KINGTON LANGLEY CROQUET CLUB
Kington Langley Croquet Club Playing Field, Church Road, Kington Langley, Wilts.

72 LANSDOWN CROQUET CLUB
Lansdown Croquet Club Northfields, Lansdown, Bath, Avon.

73 LEICESTER CROQUET CLUB
Leicester Croquet Club Victoria Park, London Road, Leicester.

74 LETCHWORTH CROQUET CLUB
Letchworth Croquet Club

75 LITTLETON CROQUET CLUB
Littleton Croquet Club Littleton, Winchester, Hants.

76 LLOYD'S CROQUET SOCIETY
Lloyd's Croquet Society Lloyd's, London EC3

77 LOUGHBOROUGH CROQUET CLUB
Loughborough Croquet Club Loughborough Technical College, Forest Road, Loughborough, Leics.

78 LYM VALLEY CROQUET CLUB
Lym Valley Croquet Club

79 METEOROLOGICAL OFFICE CROQUET CLUB
Meteorological Office CC Met. Office, Room 304, London Road, Bracknell, Berks.

80 NAILSEA CROQUET CLUB
Nailsea Croquet Club Kenford Park, Birdlip Close, Nailsea, Bristol.

81 NEWARK CROQUET CLUB
Newark Croquet Club

82 NEWPORT CROQUET CLUB
Newport Croquet Club

83 NORTHAMPTON CROQUET
CLUB
Northampton Croquet Club

84 NORTON HALL CROQUET CLUB
Norton Hall Croquet Club Imperial
Chemical Industries, Norton Hall,
Norton-on-Tees, Cleveland.

85 NORWICH CROQUET CLUB
Norwich Croquet Club Slough-
bottom Park,
Hellesden Hall Road, off Drayton
Road, Norwich, Norfolk.

86 NOTTINGHAM CROQUET CLUB
Nottingham Croquet Club High-
field, University Boulevard, Nottingham.

87 ORMESBY HALL CROQUET
CLUB
Ormesby Hall Croquet Club
Ormesby Hall, Middlesborough,
Teeside.

88 OTTERY ST. MARY ASSOCIA-
TION CROQUET CLUB
Ottery St. Mary ACC

89 PARSONS GREEN CLUB
Parsons Green Club Broomhouse
Lane, Fulham, London SW6

90 PENDLE CROQUET CLUB
Pendle Croquet Club Nelson &
Colne College,
Scotland Road, Nelson, Lancs.

91 PHYLLIS COURT CLUB
Phyllis Court Club Marlow Road,
Henley-on-Thames, Oxon. RG9
2HT

92 PIRELLI & GENERAL SOCIAL &
SPORTS CLUB
Pirelli & General S & S Club Dew
Lane, Eastleigh, Hants.

93 PLYMOUTH CROQUET CLUB
Plymouth Croquet Club

94 PRESTON LAWNS LT &
CROQUET CLUB
Preston Lawns LT & Croquet Club
Preston Drive, Brighton, E. Sussex.

95 RAMSGATE CROQUET CLUB
Ramsgate Croquet Club The West-
cliff Lawns, Royal Esplanade, Ramsgate, Kent.

96 READING CROQUET CLUB
Reading Croquet Club Palmer Park,
Reading, Berks.

97 REIGATE PRIORY CROQUET
CLUB
Reigate Priory Croquet Club Reigate
Priory Cricket Club, Park Lane,
Reigate, Surrey.

98 RIPON CROQUET CLUB
Ripon Croquet Club

99 ROEHAMPTON CLUB
The Roehampton Club Roehampton
Lane, London SW15 5LR

100 ROTTINGDEAN CROQUET
CLUB
Rottingdean Croquet Club Kipling
Gardens, The Green, Rottingdean,
E. Sussex.

101 RYDE LAWN TENNIS &
CROQUET CLUB
Ryde Lawn Tennis & Croquet Club
Playstreet Lane, Ryde, Isle of Wight.

102 SALISBURY CROQUET CLUB
Salisbury Croquet Club

103 SHREWSBURY CROQUET CLUB
Shrewsbury Croquet Club Monk-
moor Recreation Ground, Shrewsbury, Shropshire.

104 SIDMOUTH LT & CROQUET CLUB
Sidmouth LT & Croquet Club Fortfield Terrace, Sidmouth, Devon
EX10 8NT

105 SOUTH DERBYSHIRE CROQUET CLUB
South Derbyshire Croquet Club

106 SOUTH EAST ESSEX CROQUET CLUB
South East Essex Croquet Club

107 SOUTHPORT CROQUET CLUB
Southport Croquet Club Victoria Park, Rotten Row, Southport, Merseyside.

108 SOUTHWELL CROQUET CLUB
Southwell Croquet Club Kelham Hall, Newark, Notts.

109 STAFFORD CROQUET CLUB
Stafford Croquet Club Rowley Park Stadium, Highfields, Stafford.

110 STOCKEY FURZEN CRICKET & CROQUET CLUB
Stockey Furzen C & Croquet Club Gidleigh Park, Chagford, Devon
TQ13 8HH

111 STOKE CROQUET CLUB
Stoke Croquet Club Victoria Park, Tunstall, Stoke-on-Trent, Staffs.

112 STOURBRIDGE CROQUET CLUB
Stourbridge Croquet Club Mary Stevens Park, Stourbridge, W. Midlands.

113 ST. ALBANS CROQUET CLUB
St. Albans Croquet Club Clarence Park, St Albans, Herts.

114 SURBITON CROQUET CLUB
Surbiton Croquet Club Alexandra Drive, Surbiton, Surrey.

115 SUSSEX COUNTY CROQUET & LT CLUB
Sussex County Croquet & LT Club Victoria Road, Southwick, Brighton, E. Sussex.

116 SWINDON CROQUET CLUB
Swindon Croquet Club

117 SYDENHAM LT & CROQUET CLUB
Sydenham LT & Croquet Club Lawrie Park Road, London SE26

118 TAUNTON DEANE CROQUET CLUB
Taunton Deane Croquet Club Taunton, Somerset.

119 THAMESIDE CROQUET CLUB
Thameside Croquet Club Bishops Palace, Fulham, London SW6

120 THOMAS COOK SPORTS & SOCIAL CLUB
Thomas Cook S & S Club P.O. Box 36, Thorpe Wood, Peterborough
PE3 6SB

121 TRACY PARK GOLF & COUNTRY CLUB
Tracy Park Golf & Country Club Wick, Bristol.

122 TUNBRIDGE WELLS CROQUET CLUB
Tunbridge Wells Croquet Club Shemfold Park, Frant, Tunbridge Wells, Kent.

123 TYNESIDE CROQUET CLUB
Tyneside Croquet Club Smith's Park, North Shields, Tyne & Wear.

124 VINE ROAD CROQUET CLUB
Vine Road Croquet Club

125 WALSALL CROQUET CLUB
Walsall Croquet Club The Aboretum, Walsall, W. Midlands.

126 **WEAR VALLEY CROQUET CLUB**
Wear Valley Croquet Club

127 **WELLCOME FOUNDATION LTD CROQUET CLUB**
Wellcome Foundation Ltd CC High Street, Dartford, Kent.

128 **WELLCOME RESEARCH CROQUET CLUB**
Wellcome Research CC Wellcome Research Labs., Langley Court, South Eden Park Road, Beckenham, Kent BR3 3BS

129 **WELLINGTON CROQUET CLUB**
Wellington Croquet Club Wellington, Somerset.

130 **WELLS PALACE CROQUET CLUB**
Wells Palace Croquet Club The Bishop's Palace, Wells, Somerset.

131 **WELLS PRIORY CROQUET CLUB**
Wells Priory Croquet Club

132 **WERRINGTON CROQUET CLUB (PETERBOROUGH)**
Werrington Croquet Club Werrington Sports Centre, Peterborough, Cambs.

133 **WINCHESTER TENNIS & SQUASH CLUB**
Winchester LT & Squash Club Bereweeke Road, Winchester, Hants. SO22 6AP

134 **WOKING LT & CROQUET CLUB**
Woking LT & Croquet Club Pine Road, Hook Heath, Woking, Surrey.

135 **WOLVERHAMPTON CROQUET CLUB**
Wolverhampton Croquet Club The Recreation Ground, Church Road, Bradmore, Wolverhampton, W. Midlands.

136 **WORCESTER CROQUET CLUB**
Worcester Croquet Club Stonehall Farm, Green Street, Kempsey, Worcester WR5 3QB

137 **WORTHING CROQUET CLUB**
Worthing Croquet Club Hill Barn, Hill Barn Lane, Worthing, W. Sussex.

138 **WREST PARK CROQUET CLUB**
Wrest Park Croquet Club Nat. Inst. of Ag. Eng., Wrest Park, Silsoe, Beds.

139 **YELVERTON CROQUET CLUB**
Yelverton Croquet Club

140 **YORK CROQUET CLUB**
York Croquet Club Beningbrough Hall, Beningbrough, York.

B. *Affiliated Schools & Universities*

1 **ARDINGLY COLLEGE**
Ardingly College Ardingly, W. Sussex.

2 **BEACHBOROUGH SCHOOL**
Beachborough School Westbury, Brackley, Northants. NN13 5LB

3 **BEDFORD MODERN SCHOOL**
Bedford Modern School Manton Lane, Bedford MK41 7NT

4 **BIRMINGHAM UNIVERSITY**
Birmingham University

5 **BISHOP VESEY'S GRAMMAR SCHOOL**
Bishop Vesey's Grammar School Sutton Coldfield, W. Midlands B74 3NH

6 **CAMBRIDGE UNIVERSITY**
Cambridge University

7 **COLCHESTER ROYAL GRAMMAR SCHOOL**
Colchester Royal Grammar School Lexden Road, Colchester, Essex CO2 3ND

8 DUBLIN UNIVERSITY
Dublin University Trinity College,
College Green, Dublin 2, Eire.

9 DULWICH COLLEGE
Dulwich College Dulwich, London
SE21 7LD

10 DURHAM UNIVERSITY
Durham University D. U. Athletic
Union, New Elvet, Durham City,
Durham.

11 FARNHAM COLLEGE
Farnham College Morley Road,
Farnham, Surrey GU9 8LU

12 FETTES COLLEGE
Fettes College Carrington Road,
Edinburgh EH4 1QX

13 HEATHFIELD SCHOOL
Heathfield School Ascot, Berks. SL5
8BQ

14 ICKNIELD HIGH SCHOOL
Icknield High School Riddy Lane,
Luton, Beds. LU3 2AH

15 LUDLOW COLLEGE
Ludlow College Ludlow, Shropshire
SY8 1BE

16 MANCHESTER GRAMMAR
SCHOOL
Manchester Grammar School Man-
chester M13 0XT

17 MILLFIELD SCHOOL
Millfield School Shepton Mallet,
Somerset.

18 NAILSEA COMPREHENSIVE
SCHOOL
Nailsea Comprehensive School
Mizzymead Road, Nailsea, Bristol
BS19 2HN

19 NEWCASTLE UNIVERSITY
Newcastle University Kings Walk,
Newcastle-upon-Tyne, Tyne & Wear
NE1 8QB

20 NOTTINGHAM UNIVERSITY
Nottingham University c/o Athletic
Union, Portland Building, Uni-
versity Park, Nottingham.

21 OXFORD POLYTECHNIC
Oxford Polytechnic

22 OXFORD UNIVERSITY
Oxford University The Parks,
Oxford.

23 POUND HILL MIDDLE SCHOOL
Pound Hill Middle School Crawley
Lane, Pound Hill, Crawley,
W. Sussex.

24 QUEEN ELIZABETH GRAMMAR
SCHOOL
Queen Elizabeth Grammar School
Blackburn, Lancs.

25 READING UNIVERSITY
Reading University

26 SETTLE HIGH SCHOOL
Settle High School Settle, N. Yorks.
BD24 0AU

27 ST. ANDREWS UNIVERSITY
St. Andrews University St. Andrews,
Fife, Scotland.

28 STOWE SCHOOL
Stowe School Buckingham, Bucks.

29 TAUNTON J. S. SCHOOL
Taunton J. S. School Staplegrove
Road, Taunton, Somerset.

30 TUDOR GRANGE
Tudor Grange Dingle Lane, Solihull,
W. Midlands.

31 UNIVERSITY OF LONDON
University Of London

32 VARNDEAN SIXTH FORM
COLLEGE
Varndean Sixth Form College
Brighton, E. Sussex BN1 6WQ

33 VERDIN COMPREHENSIVE SCHOOL
Verdin Comprehensive School High Street, Winsford, Cheshire.

34 WOLVERHAMPTON GRAMMAR SCHOOL
Wolverhampton Grammar School Compton Road, Wolverhampton WV3 9RB

35 WORTH SCHOOL
Worth School Paddock Hurst Road, Turners Hill, Crawley, W. Sussex RH10 4SO

36 WREKIN COLLEGE
Wrekin College Sutherland Avenue, Wellington, Telford, Shropshire TF1 3BG

Hotels with Croquet Lawns

Berystede Hotel
Bagshot Road
Ascot
Berks
SL5 9JH

Cairn Hotel
Ripon Road
Harrogate
Yorkshire
HG1 2JD

Copthorne Hotel
Copthorne
West Sussex
RH10 3PG

Court Barn Country House Hotel
Clawton
Holsworthy
Devon
EX22 6PS

Fosse Manor Hotel
Stow on the Wold
Gloucester
GL54 1JX

Grand Island Hotel
Ramsey
Isle of Man

Hotel Plas Penhelig
Aberdovey
Gwynedd
LL35 ONA

Hydro Hotel
St John's Road
Eastbourne
East Sussex
BN20 9NR

Murray Arms Hotel
Gatehouse-of-Fleet
Castle Douglas
Dumfries and Galloway
Scotland
DG7 2HY

Nivingstone House Country Hotel
Cleish
Tayside
Scotland
KY13 7LS

Oatlands Park Hotel
146 Oatlands Drive
Weybridge
Surrey
KT13 9HB

Penmere Manor Hotel
Mongleath Road
Falmouth
Cornwall
TR11 4PN

Rookery Hall Hotel
Worleston
Nantwich
Cheshire
CW5 6DQ

Swallow Hotel
Old Shire Lane
Waltham Abbey
Essex
EN9 3LX

Taychreggan Hotel
Taynuit
Strathclyde
Scotland
PA35 1HQ

Tolcarne Hotel
Tintagel Road
Boscastle
Cornwall PL35 OAS
Tel: 08405 654

Underscar Hotel
Applethwaite
Keswick
Cumbria

AMERICA

The Breakers
One, South County Road,
Palm Beach
Florida 33480

Blantyre Hotel
Blantyre
Lenox
Massachusetts

Columbia Lakes Country Club
Columbia Lakes Country Resort
188 Freeman Boulevard
West Columbia

Erawan Garden Hotel
76–477 Highway 111
Indian Wells
California

Gasparilla Inn and Cottages
Gasparilla Island, Boca Grande
Florida 33921
Tel (813) 964 2201

The Inn at Rancho Sante Fe
PO Box 869
Ranch Sante Fe
California

La Mancha Resort
444 Avanida Caballeros
Palm Springs
California

Meadowood Resort and Country
Club
900 Meadowood Lane
St Helena
CA 94574

Palm Beach Polo and Country Club
13198 West Forest Hill Boulevard
West Palm Beach
Florida 33414

APPENDIX 2

British Open Championship Winners: 1867 – 1990

1867 W. J. Whitmore
1868 W. H. Peel
1869 G. C. Joad
1870 W. H. Peel
1871 W. H. Peel
1872 C. Black
1873 J. D. Heath
1874 J. D. Heath
1875 R. Gray
1876 Colonel Busk
1877 B. C. Evelegh
1878 A. H. E. Spong
1881 A. H. E. Spong
1882 A. H. E. Spong (won the cup outright. Championship lapsed until 1897)
1897 C. E. Willis
1898 Rev. C. Powell
1899 B. C. Evelegh
1900 J. E. Austin
1901 R. N. Roper
1902 C. Corbally
1903 C. Corbally
1904 R. C. J. Beaton
1905 Miss L. Gower (later Mrs R. Beaton)

1906 C. Corbally
1907 R. C. J. Beaton
1908 C. Corbally
1909 G. Ashmore
1910 C. L. O'Callaghan
1911 E. Whitaker
1912 C. L. O'Callaghan
1913 C. Corbally
1914 P. D. Mathews (1915 – 1918 no competition)
1919 P. D. Mathews
1920 P. D. Mathews
1921 C. L. O'Callaghan
1922 C. E. Pepper
1923 H. W. J. Snell
1924 D. L. G. Joseph
1925 Miss D. D. Steel
1926 B. C. Apps
1927 P. D. Mathews
1928 K. H. Coxe
1929 Lt.-Colonel W. B. du Pré
1930 B. C. Apps
1931 B. C. Apps
1932 H. O. Hicks
1933 Miss D. D. Steel
1934 Lt.-Colonel W. B. du Pré

1935	Miss D. D. Steel	1965	J. W. Solomon
1936	Miss D. D. Steel	1966	J. W. Solomon
1937	C. F. Colman	1967	J. W. Solomon
1938	D. J. V. Hamilton-Miller	1968	J. W. Solomon
1939	H. O. Hicks (1940 – 1945 no competition)	1969	G. N. Aspinall
		1970	K. F. Wylie
1946	D. J. V. Hamilton-Miller	1971	K. F. Wylie
1947	H. O. Hicks	1972	Prof. B. G. Neal
1948	H. O. Hicks	1973	Prof. B. G. Neal
1949	H. O. Hicks	1974	G. N. Aspinall
1950	H. O. Hicks	1975	G. N. Aspinall
1951	G. L. Reckitt	1976	G. N. Aspinall
1952	H. O. Hicks	1977	M. E. W. Heap
1953	J. W. Solomon	1978	G. N. Aspinall
1954	A. G. F. Ross (New Zealand)	1979	D. K. Openshaw
1955	E. P. C. Cotter	1980	W. B. Prichard
1956	J. W. Solomon	1981	D. K. Openshaw
1957	Dr W. R. D. Wiggins	1982	G. N. Aspinall
1958	E. P. C. Cotter	1983	G. N. Aspinall
1959	J. W. Solomon	1984	G. N. Aspinall
1960	Mrs Hope Rotherham	1985	D. K. Openshaw
1961	J. W. Solomon	1986	J. K. Hogan (New Zealand)
1962	E. P. C. Cotter	1987	M. N. Avery
1963	J. W. Solomon	1988	S. N. Mulliner
1964	J. W. Solomon	1989	J. K. Hogan (New Zealand)
		1990	S. N. Mulliner

Important Dates In The History of English Croquet

1867 First major 'official' tournament, later called The Open Championships.

1868 Whitmore publishes his *Croquet Tactics*, the first comprehensive analysis of the scientific nature of the game.

1869 Foundation of the All England Croquet Club.

1870 Wimbledon opened as a ground for the All England Croquet Club at Worple Road. Tight Croquet (placing a foot on the striker's ball) was banned.
Boxwood balls were introduced as regulation.

1871 Height of the peg was standardized at eighteen inches.

1872 Size of the hoops was reduced to three and three quarter inches.

1882 Croquet no longer played at Wimbledon, the game began to go into decline.

1894 Beginning of a revival with a national tournament held at Lock's Meadow, Maidstone.

1896 Croquet revived at Wimbledon.

1897 United All England Croquet Association (UAECA) founded.

The size of the court was reduced to thirty-five by twenty-eight yards.

1899 The end faces of mallets were to be parallel and of the same size and shape.

1900 The UAECA changed its name to the Croquet Association (CA).

1902 Roehampton became the headquarters of the CA.

1904 The first edition of the *Croquet Gazette*.
Top of the first hoop was painted blue.

1905 Introduction of corner pegs (invented four years earlier by J. E. Austin, proponent of the 'scythe' mallet).

1910 The Croquet Association moved its offices from 47 Fleet Street to 4 Southampton Row.

1911 Ruled that mallet could not be changed more than once during a game (except when genuinely damaged).

1912 The committee of the Croquet Association was re-named the Council.

1922 The Willis setting (using one peg in the middle of the game instead of two as in the Hale setting) was adopted.

1924 Top of the rover (final) hoop was painted red.

1925 MacRoberston Shield competition inaugurated – the first 'Test match'.

1929 White pegs were introduced to be used as 'bisques' (free turns). These had previously been denoted by the use of coins.

1936 D. D. Steel became the first (and only) woman to win the Open Championships four times.

1947 Detachable top added to the peg.

1952 Queen Elizabeth II grants patronage of CA.

1959 CA offices move from 4 Southampton Row to Hurlingham Club.

1967 Queen visits Hurlingham.

1972 Laws of croquet redrafted (second time since 1961).

1984 Laws re–drafted.

1989 Laws re-drafted.

1990 Decision to include USA in next Test series.

Select Bibliography

1868 *Croquet Tactics*, W. J. Whitmore, H. Cox

1870 *The Game of Croquet, Its Laws and Regulations*, de la Rue

1872 *The Book of Croquet: Its Tactics, Laws and Mode of Play*, Arthur Lillie, Jaques

1897 *Croquet, Its History, Rules and Secrets*, Arthur Lillie, Longmans, Green and Co

1899 *The Sportman's Yearbook*, Lawrence and Bullen Limited

1899 *Croquet*, Leonard B. Williams, Isthmian Library

1900 *Croquet Up to Date*, Arthur Lillie, Longmans Green and Co

1900 *Croquet*, The Hon H. C. Needham, Bell

1914 *Croquet*, Lord Tollemache, Stanley Paul and Co Ltd

1923 *Croquet: Hints on Practice, Tactics and Stroke Play*, Lord Tollemache, Phillipson and Golder

1930 *Croquet and How to Play It*, A. G. F. Ross, Wedderspoon

1932 *The Art of Croquet*, H. F., Crowther-Smith, The Sports and Pastimes Library, H. F. and G. Witherby

1937 *A Handbook On Modern Croquet*, with a foreword by the Viscount Doneraile, Longmans Green and Co

1939 *Practical Lawn Craft and Management of Sports Turf*, R. B. Dawson (sixth edition revised published in 1968) Crosby Lockwood and Son Ltd

1947 *Modern Croquet, Tips and Practice*, Lord Tollemache, Strange the Printers Limited, Eastbourne, East Sussex

1949 *Croquet, A Handbook on the Strokes and Tactics of the Game* (reprinted from 1910), G. F. Handel Elvey, John Jaques and Son, Thornton Heath, Surrey

1954 *Croquet Today*, M. B. Reckitt, Macdonald

1960 *Tackle Croquet This Way*, E. P. C. Cotter, Stanley Paul and Co Ltd

1961 *A Rush on the Ultimate*, H. R. F. Keating, Victor Gollancz (published by Penguin Books, 1966)

1966 *Croquet and How to Play It*, D. Miller and R. Thorp, Faber and Faber

1966 *Croquet*, J. W. Solomon, B. T. Batsford Ltd (republished in 1983 by E P Publishing Ltd and in 1989 in paperback by A and C Black

1973 *Croquet*, National Westminster Bank Sport Coaching Series (introduction by Roger Bray)

1981 *The History of Croquet*, D. M. C. Prichard, Cassell Limited

1987 *The World of Croquet*, John McCullough and Stephen Mulliner, The Crowood Press

1989 *Simply Teach Yourself Croquet*, Peter Danks, The Shillingate Press

1989 *How to Play Croquet, A Step by Step Guide* (foreword by Nigel Aspinall), Mike Shaw, Jarrold Colour Publications

1989 *Play The Game, Croquet*, Stephen Mulliner, Ward Lock Limited, London

1989 *Townsend's Croquet Almanack*, Townsend Croquet Ltd

1990 *Townsend's Croquet Almanack*, Townsend Croquet Ltd

INDEX